AUSTRIA

TIME-LIFE BOOKS/AMSTERDAM

COOKERY AROUND THE WORLD
AUSTRIA

ADELHEID BEYREDER

Food photography: Michael Brauner

Germany

Upper Austria

Vorarlberg

Tyrol

Salzburg

Switzerland

East
Tyrol

Carinthia

Italy

CONTENTS

Czechoslovakia

wer Austria

Vienna

Hungary

tyria   Burgenland

Slovenia

AUSTRIA: LAND OF LAKES AND MOUNTAINS

Austria is one of the smallest countries in Europe, yet one of its most popular and well-loved holiday destinations. So numerous and varied are its attractions that the tourist season extends throughout the year, embracing all four seasons. In winter, dedicated skiers and climbers are drawn to the many superb alpine resorts; in spring and summer, the gently rolling plains and alpine foothills are perfect walking country, and the beautiful lakes, warmed by the sun, play host to watersports enthusiasts and holidaying families. And in autumn, the grape harvest is a focus for all wine lovers. Year-round, the romantic capital, Vienna, enchants lovers of art and music, and countless other towns delight visitors with their rich heritage of castles, medieval burghers' houses and Baroque churches and palaces, all in picturesque settings.

Many of the visitors to this charming country will share one common passion: the legendary Austrian cuisine. Austrians are great lovers of food, and take great pride in the culinary experiences their country has to offer visitors. Whether a tourist chooses to sample the famous boiled beef dish, *Tafelspitz*, in the elegant surroundings of Vienna's famous Hotel Sacher, or prefers simply to linger a while in one of the city's many coffee houses, indulging in a delicious pastry with a *Kapuziner, Türkisher* or *Melange*—one of Vienna's many speciality coffees—there is something to suit the most robust appetite or the sweetest tooth. For those who prefer the peace of the countryside, there are the simple, leisurely delights of sitting with a local wine-grower, sampling a glass of his new vintage, or lunching on a hearty spread of smoked meats, cheeses and cider in a rustic inn.

Cooking has always been a highly valued skill in Austria—where else would there be so many different ways to serve whipped cream with coffee?—and is practised with relish by experts and amateurs alike. This book endeavours to evoke the flavour of the country, its peoples and its food by showing you how to cook Austrian dishes in your own kitchen.

The first chapter introduces the country's different regions, and outlines their scenic attractions, local specialities and cultural events. Then follow six sections of authentic recipes, ordered as they would appear on a menu—from hearty soups and light snacks to the desserts and pastries for which Austria is famed. They are accompanied by easy-to-follow, step-by-step instructions. and are interspersed with short information boxes on some of the more important ingredients. The recipes are followed by menu suggestions for both family and more festive meals, and, finally, a glossary explaining some of the less familiar terms, ingredients and dishes found in Austrian cuisine.

It is always an adventure to explore the cookery of another country—so consider this book your invitation to see, smell and re-create at home the authentic cuisine of Austria.

CROSSROADS
OF EUROPE

Austria has had a long and turbulent history, much of which can be directly attributed to its geographical situation. Located at the heart of Europe, at the intersection of six other nations, it has for centuries served as a busy crossroads on traffic routes between east and west, north and south, subject to the influences of different peoples and cultures.

The pattern of settlement in Austria has largely been shaped by its alpine environment. Some 2,000 years ago, the Romans forged a way through the Alps and along the Danube to establish a settlement where Vienna is today. In their wake, following the decline of the Roman Empire, came a long, unsettled period of territorial disputes and invasions by barbaric hordes, until, in the 10th century, Austria's first ruling house established itself in Vienna.

The city grew in importance as a trading post and when, at the end of the 13th century, Count Rudolf of Hapsburg assumed power, the stage was set for an era of growth and prosperity lasting six centuries. By controlling the two important alpine passes and the Vienna basin, the Hapsburgs built up a great empire that at one time or another embraced Poles, Hungarians, Czechs, Romanians, Italians, Serbs, Croats, Dutch, Spanish, French and Swiss, and as many as 16 different languages.

The golden epoch for which Vienna is famed began around 1600 and lasted until the end of the 18th century. It was an age of exuberance, which saw the flowering of music, theatre, Baroque architecture and, not least, the grand, ostentatious cuisine that was such a feature of the life of the aristocracy and which found fame around the world.

Austria today comprises nine federal provinces. To the east lies Burgenland, with its prairie-like landscape and almost Mediterranean climate; here sits the Neusiedler lake, Austria's lowest-lying point. The landscape of Upper and Lower Austria includes not only mountain peaks, rolling hills and lush woodlands, but also fertile lowland regions such as the Mühlviertel and the Weinviertel, where vines flourish. Austria's western mountains reach heights of up to 3,000 metres, their lower slopes given over to pasture. In the south are the charming provinces of Carinthia and Styria, with their high peaks, gentle hills and numerous lakes.

Each of these provinces has a distinct linguistic and culinary identity, the result of their nation's diverse population and centuries of cultural interchange. Although Viennese-style cuisine—essentially that created during the heyday of the Austro-Hungarian Empire—tends to predominate, each region clings fiercely to its individual identity, jealously preserving local specialities, preparation methods, festivals and traditions.

Burgenland: Garden of Vienna

Burgenland—the "Land of Castles"—Austria's most easterly province, is a narrow strip of land comprising two quite different types of territory: the eastern part is dominated by the great open plains of the *puszta* (prairie land), and the hilly, wooded south by gentle hills and fertile pasture land. The climate is mild and dry, providing perfect growing conditions not only for the province's many vineyards, but for other sun-loving crops such as figs, almonds, peaches, apricots and herbs. In the *puszta* lies Europe's only steppe lake, the mysterious Neusiedler See, whose warm, shallow, reed-fringed waters are a haven for more than 250 species of birds—not to mention the watersports enthusiasts who also flock here throughout the year.

The historic capital, Eisenstadt, is the smallest of the provincial capitals, and is famous for its association with Joseph Haydn (1732-1809), who for 30 years was employed here as *Kapellmeister*. The composer's patron was the Hungarian aristocrat Prince Nikolaus Esterhazy, whose family built the great Baroque palace which bears their name, and which dominates the town skyline today.

In addition to the numerous castles that gave the province its name, Burgenland has charming mountain villages which in the summertime take on an almost Mediterranean air, their dazzling, whitewashed one-storey houses set off by red oleander shrubs and dried bundles of corn on the cob. Many of them are situated in the wine-producing areas and are especially popular with tourists during the autumn grape harvest. The best time to see the wine village of Donnerskirchen, however, is during mid-April to early May, when the white blossom of thousands of cherry trees provides a spectacular natural backdrop. One town well worth visiting—and famous for its red wine—is Rust, where the well-preserved Renaissance and Baroque burghers' houses have storks nesting on their roofs in summer.

The cuisine of Burgenland is strongly Hungarian in flavour, for the province formed part of Hungary from 1648 until 1921. One lavish dessert of Hungarian ancestry is the famous *Somloer Nockerln*, made from light and dark sponge cake, hot vanilla sauce, whipped cream and chocolate. Some of the province's many castles have been turned into luxury hotels and restaurants: at Lockenhaus Castle, for example, you can indulge in a meal including such rich dishes as bread fried in dripping, herb strudel, sucking pig, and yeast dumplings, rounded off by *Grammelpogatscherln*—little yeast pastries with pork crackling and caraway seeds—delicious with Burgenlander wine. At Bernstein Castle, you can feast on local delicacies in what was once the knights' hall.

On the last Friday in August, the Esterhazy Palace hosts Austria's most important wine fair, the Festival of 1,000 Wines. This ten-day event takes place in the castle's Orangery and its enchanting grounds. The feast of St Martin, patron saint of the province, is celebrated on 11 November with wine-naming and wine-tasting ceremonies and the traditional hearty peasant meal of crispy roast goose with red cabbage and dumplings.

The sunny waters of Carinthia's lakes, of which there are more than a hundred, frequently enjoy temperatures as high as 27° C.

Carinthia: Sunny Lakes and Spas

Carinthia, bordering on Italy and Slovenia, is Austria's most southerly, and therefore sunniest, province. It lies in a basin surrounded by mountains, most notably the magnificent crests of the northern Hohe Tauern range—which includes the country's highest peak, the Großglockner—and the long westerly chain of the Carnic Alps, a haven for climbers, walkers and skiers.

Lovers of more leisurely pursuits are drawn to the interior, much of which is forested, and to the many spas and warm alpine lakes. Among the best known are the Millstätter See, the Ossiacher See and the largest, the Wörther See, near whose shores lies the ancient provincial capital, Klagenfurt. This handsome Baroque city, with its distinctly Mediterranean feel, is the home of one of Austria's most famous pastry shops, *Musil,* where you can enjoy exquisite tortes and other sweet delicacies.

Foremost among the culinary specialities of Carinthia are its game and fish, the latter to be found in abundance in the numerous tributary streams of the Drau, which meanders through the region. A typical local speciality are *Nudeln*—small, folded pasta squares stuffed with a variety of fillings. These are named according to their filling; for example, *Fleischnudeln* (meat), *Specknudeln* (bacon), and *kasnudeln* (quark). *Kletzennudeln,* with their filling of dried pears, are delicious served as a sweet with sugar and melted butter on top.

A particularly authentic Carinthian snack—known locally as *Vesper* or *Brotzeit,* and usually served on a wooden platter—consists of country ham, dry sausage, cheese and fresh black bread. Also good with black bread is *Verhackerte,* a spread of finely chopped bacon seasoned with pepper,

Eisenstadt, with only 11,000 inhabitants, is Austria's smallest provincial capital. Its charming Baroque church, one of the station churches, is regularly visited by processions of pilgrims.

important and ancient annual fairs is the *Wiesenmarkt,* or Meadow Market, which is held at St Veit an der Glan on 29 September, the feast of St Michael. For villages throughout the Lavant Valley, the October harvest festival is a popular celebratory occasion.

Lower Austria: Green Valley of the Danube

The range of scenic contrasts that makes Austria so appealing are all to be found in Lower Austria, the country's largest province: from the majestic River Danube and its many tributaries, flanked by vine-clad terraces, to dense woodland, sweeping planes, gently sloping hills and 2,000-metre-high mountains.

At the heart of Lower Austria, in a basin surrounded by a great swathe of woodland (the Vienna Woods), lies the state capital, Vienna, which became a separate federal province of Austria in 1920. Only as recently as 1986 did the people of Lower Austria elect their own capital, the Baroque city of St Pölten.

A combination of a mild climate and fertile loess soil have attracted settlers to this region since prehistoric times. It was here that the 25,000-year-old carved limestone figure known as the Venus of Willendorf was unearthed, in a stretch of the Danube Valley known as the Wachau, today a maze of ancient market towns, romantic castles and thriving vineyards.

Agriculture plays a vital part in the region's economy. In the well-watered lowlands, such as the Wachau or the Weinviertel, vines have been cultivated since Celtic times, but it was the

A neat patchwork of immaculately groomed fields crisscrosses the gentle slopes of the Traunviertel in Upper Austria, a favourite spot for ramblers.

salt and garlic—also a speciality of neighbouring Styria. Other regional specialities include dried sausages, smoked meats, bacon, honey and *Kloatzenbrot,* the local fruit loaf.

Meals are typically accompanied by strong country cider—usually made from apples, but often from pears—or *Obstler,* a clear fruit schnapps. In addition to cider, Carinthians enjoy such exotic drinks as fruit, juniper-berry, or spruce, schnapps, raspberry or pine spirit, and highly alcoholic rum.

As in other regions of Austria, fairs are held all year round in this province, to commemorate such events as the wine harvest, or the dedication of a town or its church. One of the most

Dressed in traditional costume, two young citizens of Dürnstein in Lower Austria enjoy one of their region's many festivals.

Romans who first turned winemaking into a commercial venture. On the intensively cultivated plains, such as the Marchfeld ("the granary of Austria"), wheat, vegetables, sugar beet and sunflowers thrive.

The Danube Valley is one of Europe's most popular holiday destinations, not only for its architectural splendours and beautiful countryside—a visit in springtime, when the apricot trees are in blossom, is an unforgettable experience—but also for its excellent wines, first-class restaurants and rustic inns. There are numerous attractions, many centred around the centuries-old wine industry. The Kellergasse (wine-cellar lane) in Falkenstein is the home of Austria's oldest wine cellars; although unused for many years, they are well preserved. And the ancient walled town of Retz has 20 km of underground cellars and tunnels dating from the 15th century. To accompany the local

wine, try the hearty *Weinviertler Schlachtplatte*, a substantial spread of black pudding, liver sausage, bratwurst and boiled ham—traditionally made from very fresh pork—and shredded, pickled cabbage (sauerkraut).

Throughout the region, St Martin's Day (11 November) is commemorated with roast goose, and wines from the new vintage. On 15 November in Klosterneuburg, the feast of St Leopold, patron saint of Lower Austria, is marked by the popular *Faßlrutschen*, in which revellers slide down a giant wine cask. Austria's best-known wine-growers' event is the vintners' procession, held in Perchtoldsdorf, on the outskirts of Vienna. This 500-year-old festival takes place on the Sunday after St Leonard's Day (6 November). Among the main festivals in the Wachau are the Apricot Fair (July), harvest festival in the market town of Spitz (October), and the August Riesling Festival at Weißenkirchen.

A gentle breeze delights yachting enthusiasts on the romantic Traunsee, one of the larger lakes in the Salzkammergut and a popular holiday destination.

Upper Austria: "Province on the Enns"

Like neighbouring Lower Austria, this region offers the visitor topographical diversity and stunning natural features. In the north, steeply wooded slopes extend along the fertile valleys of the Mühlviertel plateau as far as the Bohemian Forest. In the west, the softly undulating hills of the Innviertel are interspersed with pleasant valleys dotted with little villages and hamlets. In the south, high mountains with imposing rocky crags tower above the romantic lakes of the Salzkammergut. And to the east, dramatic gorges split the landscape of the Eisenwurzen.

The provincial capital of Upper Austria is Linz, Austria's third largest city, and famous for its fine Baroque architecture. Today, this ancient city, originally the site of a Roman fortified camp, is a busy commercial centre.

The lakes of the Salzkammergut are a busy tourist area, rich in culinary, as well as natural, treasures: in the fashionable little spa of Bad Ischl (once the favoured summer resort of Emperor Franz Joseph I), a visit to the famous *Zauner* pastry shop, a veritable Aladdin's cave of cakes, pastries and chocolates, is a must. The little villages that surround the warm waters of the Mondsee are dotted with elegant lakeside restaurants. However, it is not only in these establishments that fine food is to be found, for a rich variety of fish—taken from the clear rivers and lakes—appears on the menus of the most modest of hostelries.

But the traditional fare of the inhabitants of Upper Austria is undoubtedly the dumpling: from large meat, bacon and liver dumplings, through light, fluffy versions made from semolina, rice or breadcrumbs, to sweet, apple, poppy seed or yeast dumplings. Innviertel is particularly renowned for its bacon dumplings, which are made by finely chopping bacon (preserved in salt rather than smoked), mixing it with breadcrumb dough and then simmering in gently boiling water. Dumplings are delicious washed down with beer or dry cider, the latter made from a mixture of apples and pears. (There is a museum devoted to the art of cidermaking at St Marienkirchen an der Polsenz.)

Of the many annual regional festivities, the most famous takes place at Schärding. The biennial Wels agricultural fair (early September) is accompanied by a large funfair. Also worth seeing are the picturesque Corpus Christi processions held on the Hallstätter See and the Traunsee.

Salzburg: Birthplace of Mozart

Both the province of Salzburg—Austria's smallest—and its wonderfully picturesque capital city, take their name, meaning "Salt Mountain", from the rich salt deposits mined here some 3,000 years ago. Mighty mountain massifs, thundering waterfalls, spray-filled gorges, crystal-clear mountain lakes, and lush pastures are but a few of its natural wonders.

The city itself, with its spectacular natural setting and well-preserved ancient buildings—the skyline is dominated by the great bulk of the Hohensalzburg Fortress—must rank as one of the most beautiful in Europe, and as such is a mecca for tourists, who flock to enjoy the visual delights as well as the legendary hospitality of the inhabitants.

Beer-brewing has a 500-year-long tradition in Salzburg, and the large beer gardens in the heart of the city are perfect for whiling away a pleasant day or a summer's evening. At the historic Augustinerbräu, there is a choice of no fewer than nine buffets, offering tempting accompaniments to the beer that is brewed on the premises. Those with a sweeter tooth, who have the good fortune to find themselves a seat on the terrace of the Café Tomaselli, may satisfy their appetite with rich pastries. If, however, your taste is for good, wholesome food in a congenial setting, you will be well catered for in

the countryside around Salzburg, where the menu offers such hearty fare as *Salzburger Hochzeitssuppe* (Salzburger wedding soup), *Bierfleisch* (beef in beer) or *Z'sammg'legte Knödel* (meat-stuffed dumplings). The fluffy sweet soufflé known as *Salzburger Nockerln* is a particularly celebrated local creation, as are the little chocolate-coated balls of marzipan and nougat cream known as *Mozartkugeln*of, a souvenir very popular with visitors to Mozart's home town.

The province keeps its customs alive with many fairs and festivals. In summer, spectacular "Samson processions", featuring huge figures of Samson which serve as fertility symbols, take place in many villages in the remote Lungau valley. The spotlight falls on the city of Salzburg in Holy Week for the Easter Festival, and again in July and August, when the world-famous Music Festival is held. The Salzburger "Dult", an event similar to

In the little town of Oberndorf, in Salzburg province, members of the guild of river boatmen, resplendent in their traditional red coats and flamboyant plumed hats, cheerfully stand to attention.

Grape harvesting in autumn on the steep terraced vineyards of Leutschach, in Styria. This province, one of Austria's prettiest wine districts, has some of the highest vineyards in the world.

Munich's Oktoberfest, is celebrated in late May or early June. On 24 September, to mark the feast of St Rupert, patron saint of the province, a large fair is held in front of the cathedral, and gunshots ring out from the Hohensalzburg Fortress to commemorate the occasion.

Styria: Austria's Lush Green Heartland

Styria, Austria's second largest province, is a land of striking scenic contrasts—and corresponding climatic diversity—brought about by a regional variance in altitude of almost 3,000 metres. It encompasses, in the northwest, the lakes of the Salzkammergut and the high, varied alps of the Dachstein and, on the southern border, the gentle, vine-clad lowlands of the wine-growing area. The provincial capital, Graz—Austria's second largest town—has an ancient, well-preserved city centre, noted for a number of fine Italianate buildings. Rising above the town is a steep, wooded hill known as the Schloßberg, on top of which stands a 16th-century belfry visible for miles around.

Among Styria's natural treasures are breathtaking alpine passes, gorges and waterfalls, and stalactitic caves. Sights well worth seeing are the Styrian "Apple Route", which wends its way through splendid orchards—much of whose crop is used to make cider—and the wine road, at its most glorious in spring when the trees are in blossom, and later on when the woodlands take on their autumn colours. At this latter time of year, local inns are kept busy with trade from passing tourists, who like to sit in the autumn sunshine, or in the shade of a walnut tree, enjoying a glass or two of *Sturm*—the newly fermenting wine—and roast chestnuts.

To the west of Graz lies a region known as "Schilcherland", which takes its name from its distinctive rosé wine. This wine is a perfect accompaniment to *Brettljause*, a hearty local snack comprising smoked pork, little smoked sausages, smoked bacon, fried pork, finely chopped bacon spread, cheese, horseradish, boiled eggs, sweet peppers, tomatoes and country bread. Other regional dishes include *Ritschert*, a hotpot made with hulled barley, smoked meat, pulses and beans—also popular in neighbouring Carinthia— *Heidensterz*, a fried buckwheat-flour purée, and the hearty, pork-based *Klachelsuppe*.

The region around Bad Aussee, in the Styrian Salzkammergut, is the setting for Austria's greatest floral festival, the Narcissus Festival, held from mid-May to mid-June. Highlights include a large funfair, a parade of flower-bedecked cars, and a procession of boats on the Grundlsee. An annual grape harvest festival takes place in Gamlitz in October; while Klöch holds its wine celebrations every three years. A year-round attraction is the *Flascherlzug*, an old-fashioned narrow-gauge railway that runs through the Stainz valley at weekends between May and October. The passengers can fortify themselves en route in the buffet car with toast and dripping, *Bauernkrapfen* (large, plate-sized doughnuts) and the sparkling Schilcher wine.

Tyrol: Mountains and Meadows

This breathtakingly beautiful province, Austria's third largest, is primarily famous, of course, for its rugged alpine landscape, and indeed all routes into it bar one are via mountain passes. Throughout the region, icy glaciers and precipitous mountain crags are enchantingly offset by broad wooded slopes, picturesque alpine pastures, flower-bedecked meadows, and valleys of fertile fields.

The province is divided into two parts, East Tyrol being separated from North Tyrol by an area known as Alto Adige, ceded to Italy in 1919. The most popular tourist region is around the capital, Innsbruck, which sits amid a ring of towering peaks. This city is noted for its historic old town, in which are to be found such attractions as the Hofkirche (Court Church), which

This picturesque wooden water mill (right), clinging to a hillside near Mitteldorf, in eastern Tyrol, once ground grain. Today, the farmers deliver their crop to modern, more efficient processing plants.

A cheerful Tyrolese farmer proudly displays a splendid pair of cowbells following their customary blessing by the parish priest.

houses Europe's most spectacular royal mausoleum, the tomb of Emperor Maximilian I, and the famous "Golden Roof", a late Gothic oriel window with brilliant gilded tiles.

Among the region's culinary delights are *Schlutzkrapfen* (also known as *Schlipfkrapfen* or *Schlutzer*), which are similar to ravioli. Each valley makes its own version, which may be filled with sauerkraut, potatoes, spinach, meat or dried pears. They are delicious with a glass of the locally brewed beer or wine, the majority of which is produced in South Tyrol. One of the most popular desserts is *Nuischmalz*, made from cream, butter, flour and honey. A well-known East Tyrolese Christmas treat is *Blattlstock*, for which large sheets of yeast dough are sprinkled with poppy seeds, drizzled with clarified butter, then shaped and stiffened to look like icicles. *Kletzenbrot*, a fruit bread made with dried pears, prunes, figs and raisins, is a Tyrolese speciality. The fame of *Bauernspeck* ("peasants' bacon"), which is marinated for two

months in mild brine, juniper berries and other ingredients that are kept secret, then smoked, extends far beyond the borders of the Tyrol. The Tyrolese schnapps, made from gentian, or juniper berries or rowan berries (the fiery red fruit of the mountain ash), cheers up many a cold winter's evening.

The Tyrolese are a fun-loving people, noted for their love of traditional costume (still donned by many for holidays or festivals), their dancing, marksmanship, competitions, brass bands, processions—and, of course, yodelling! The famous Shrove Tuesday celebrations, held every four to five years, take place at Imst, Telfs and Nassereith. Zell am Ziller, east of Innsbruck, is the setting on the first Sunday in May for the *Gauderfest*, a carnival procession that features music, dancing and other traditional entertainments. To mark the occasion, special beer (*Gauderbier*) and spicy sausages (*Gauderwurst*) are produced. *Christkindlmärkte* (Christmas markets) are held at Imst and Innsbruck.

A painting of St George and the Dragon, and trompe l'oeil architectural embellishments, transform the exterior wall of an old farmhouse in Vorarlberg.

Vorarlberg: Austria's Alpine Dairy

Vorarlberg is Austria's most westerly province and extends from Lake Constance, across the fertile Rhine Valley, dotted with little gardens and orchards, to the Silvretta Massif, which rises more than 3,000 metres. The provincial capital is Bregenz, a pretty town built on the most easterly bay of Lake Constance, on the site of a Bronze Age Celtic settlement. The landmark of the town is the massive late 16th-century St Martin's Tower, which rises above the picturesque old streets of the Upper Town. Today, it houses a chapel and the local museum and offers stunning panoramic views of the city.

Agriculture is of great importance to the economy of this region, whose inhabitants enjoy the country's highest per capita income. The lush meadows and sweeping alpine pastures allow for intensive cattle farming—for example, Hittisau, a village in the Bregenz forest, has over a hundred privately owned pastures—which in turn feeds a flourishing dairy industry that produces three quarters of Austria's mountain cheeses, cream and butter.

Typical Vorarlberg specialities include such varied dishes as cheese *Spätzle*, a local type of pasta, and the tasty but inexpensive *Riebel*, a crumbled, sautéed semolina that can be served in sweet or savoury form; traditionally, this is enjoyed with a cup of hot white coffee. A favourite cake is the fluted, fruit-filled *Gugelhupf*; in Bregenz, this is known as *Ofenkatze* ("oven cat"), because its pre-cooked shape resembles a sleeping cat. As well as the many local cheeses, a favourite Vorarlberg tipple worth trying is the schnapps distilled from the thick sweet roots of yellow alpine gentian.

The people of the Vorarlberg cherish

The setting sun adds a delicate pink glow to the stunning crags of the Mieminger Berge, in northern Tyrol, one of many such sights to be enjoyed in this predominantly mountainous region.

Young and old alike enjoy the thrills of the famous giant Ferris wheel in Vienna's Prater amusement park. Completed in 1897, and rebuilt after the Second World War, the wheel offers a stunning panoramic view of the city.

their many local customs, boasting more brass bands than they do parishes! The region around Bregenz hosts many festivals: the first Sunday of Lent is marked by the lighting of bonfires on the hillsides and colourful processions in traditional costume, and in September and October the return of the herds from their alpine grazing lands is celebrated. The Bregenz Lake Festival, which runs from mid-July to the end of August, is renowned for the operas and operettas sumptuously presented on the world's largest floating stage. And children all over the region eagerly look forward to the July chocolate fair in Bludenz, a pretty town of Baroque buildings and pergolas.

Vienna: City of Coffee and Cakes

This romantic city, seat of the Holy Roman Emperor from 1558 to 1806, and until 1918 capital of the Austro-Hungarian Empire, is Austria's capital and smallest province. It is a city steeped in history, to which its rich cultural heritage bears witness: from the stunning Gothic cathedral, Baroque palaces, and 19th-century boulevards, to the many fine churches, museums and art galleries.

Of all the institutions for which the city is famous—the Vienna Boy's Choir, the Spanish Riding School, the New Year's Day Concert—one of the most popular is the coffee house. First introduced into the city towards the end of the 17th century, these small establishments rapidly became popular meeting places, enjoying their heyday at the turn of the century. Today, Vienna has more than 500 cafés; in settings that range from the luxurious to the bohemian, people gather to write, read, strike business deals, play chess, or simply to talk with friends over one of Vienna's many speciality coffees. Another cherished custom in Vienna is to visit the *Heuriger*; these simple rustic wine taverns, with their

In the elegant and luxurious surroundings of one of Vienna's grander coffee houses, a resident pianist enhances the atmosphere of calm gentility.

shady gardens, are found on every street, and provide a perfect spot at which to sample the new wine—the *Heuriger*—and watch the world go by.

No less popular an occupation in this city, however, is eating. Vienna enjoys a legendary culinary reputation that has its origins in the glittering era of the Hapsburg Empire, when the city's chefs were influenced by, and drew their inspiration from, all corners of that vast empire, in particular from the cuisines of Hungary, Czechoslovakia and the former Yugoslavia.

The Austrian love of meat and sweet dishes is reflected in the cuisine of its capital. Perhaps the most famous of Viennese dishes is that which bears its name, the *Wiener Schnitzel*, a veal escalope coated in breadcrumbs. But Vienna is above all renowned for its desserts and pastries, especially the much-loved *Sachertorte*, a rich chocolate sponge cake filled or coated with apricot jam and plain chocolate. As well as having a sweet tooth, the Viennese are partial to between-meals snacks—witness the numerous little street stands selling hot sausages spiced with mustard or horseradish.

Vienna still glories in its lavish celebratory occasions. On the first Thursday in February, opera lovers from all over the world converge on the city's magnificent State Opera House, transformed into a vast ballroom for the glittering Opera Ball. The Vienna Festival, held from mid-May through to mid-June, offers a vast choice of cultural events, from the traditional to the avant-garde. Two celebrations that have a more widespread popular appeal are the City Fair (April/May) and the Danube Island fair, which takes place in June. New Year's Eve is riotously celebrated in the square in front of St Stephen's Cathedral.

The splendid classical façade of Vienna's Parliament building, completed in 1883, glows in the twilight.

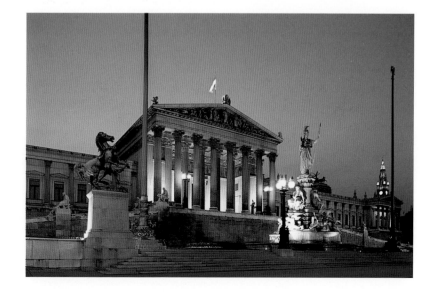

SOUPS

The Austrians hold their soups in great esteem. The unrivalled model for the substantial soups so popular today is the legendary *Olio-Suppe*. In the days of the Empire, this lavish dish was prepared once a year in the kitchens of Vienna's Hofburg Palace for the 2,000 guests at the palace ball. Among the vast quantities of ingredients used to make it were 10 kg beef, 12 kg veal, 16 calves' feet, 10 kg pork, 8 kg lamb, 8 kg game, 5 ducks, 3 geese and 10 chickens.

While nobody in Austria today cook soups on quite this scale, the variety of recipes is still such that you could serve a different soup every day of the year—from delicately flavoured broths to hearty meat and vegetable versions.

The basis of many of these soups is a strong beef broth, which can easily be prepared at home. Cover a large piece of beef with cold water and simmer, partly covered, for 3 to 4 hours, until tender, removing the scum as it forms. During the last 30 minutes add a variety of flavouring vegetables such as chopped leek, carrot and celeriac, and season with fresh, not dried, herbs: as well as the classic chives, cress, marjoram, parsley and oregano, sage and tarragon (used sparingly) are also suitable. Strain the broth and discard the vegetables. Allow to cool and skim off the fat. It is worth while making a large quantity of broth and freezing it in small quantities for later use.

Grießnockerlsuppe

Clear soup with semolina dumplings

Not difficult · Many regions

Serves 4

1 egg
about 60 g softened butter
about 120 g semolina
salt
freshly grated nutmeg
a little vegetable oil
1 bunch chives
1 litre beef broth (see page 23)

Preparation time: 45 minutes

1,200 kJ/290 calories per portion

1 Weigh the egg, then weigh out an equal amount of butter. Put the butter in a bowl and stir until creamy. Add the egg. Weigh out double the egg-weight of semolina and stir it into the butter and egg mixture, a little at a time. Season with salt and nutmeg, then leave to stand for about 5 minutes.

2 Brush a plate with oil. Using a wet teaspoon, shape the dough into oval dumplings. Place them on the plate and leave to stand in the refrigerator for about 15 minutes. Bring plenty of salted water to the boil in a wide saucepan.

3 Add the dumplings to the gently boiling water and simmer over low heat for about 10 minutes.

4 Wash the chives, shake dry and cut into tiny pieces. Heat the beef broth.

5 Remove the dumplings from the saucepan with a slotted spoon and add to the broth. Sprinkle with the chives.

Variation:
Überbackene Grießnockerln
(Baked cheese dumplings)
Make the dumplings, using 90 g butter, 3 eggs, 250 g semolina, salt and nutmeg. Preheat the oven to 220°C (425°F or Mark 7). Cook the dumplings and arrange in a buttered baking dish. Sprinkle 100 g grated cheese on top and dot with 50 g butter. Bake in the centre of the oven for 20 minutes, until golden-brown. Serve as a main dish.

Frittatensuppe

Clear soup with shredded pancake

Fairly easy • Winter dish

Serves 4

50 g flour
about 12.5 cl milk
1 egg
salt
15 g flat-leaf parsley
2 tbsp butter
1 litre beef broth (see page 23)
1 bunch chives

Preparation time: 30 minutes

740 kJ/180 calories per portion

1 Mix the flour with 2 tbsp milk, the egg and some salt in a bowl. Wash parsley, shake dry, remove the stalks and finely chop the leaves. Add to the egg mixture. Add enough milk to make a thin batter.

2 Heat a frying pan and grease with ½ tbsp butter. Ladle a quarter of the batter into the frying pan and shake, so that the batter is thinly spread over the base. Cook the pancake over low heat until golden on both sides. Repeat to make three more pancakes. If the batter becomes too thick, stir in a little more milk.

3 Roll up each pancake. Halve the pancake rolls lengthwise, then cut into shreds about 3 mm wide.

4 Heat the beef broth. Wash the chives, shake dry and cut into tiny pieces.

5 Place a portion of pancake shreds in each soup plate. Pour over the hot beef broth and sprinkle with the finely cut chives.

Leberknödelsuppe

Clear soup with liver dumplings

Serves 4

2 day-old bread rolls
½ litre milk
1 small onion
30 g butter
120 g ox liver
3 sprigs parsley
1 egg
dried marjoram
1 garlic clove
2 to 3 tbsp fresh breadcrumbs (optional)
salt · freshly ground black pepper
1 bunch chives
1 litre beef broth (see page 23)

Preparation time: 40 minutes

890 kJ/210 calories per portion

1 Soak the bread rolls in the milk. Peel and finely chop the onion. Heat the butter in a frying pan and fry the onion until transparent. Leave to cool.

2 Remove the skin and any tubes or fat from the liver. Wash, pat dry and cut into wide strips.

3 Squeeze out the bread rolls. Finely mince the liver, then the bread.

4 Wash the parsley, shake dry, remove the stalks and finely chop the leaves. Mix the liver and bread in a bowl with the fried onion. Add the egg, parsley and some marjoram. Peel and crush the garlic and stir it into the dough. If the dough is not firm enough, add some breadcrumbs. Season with salt and

pepper. Cover the dough and leave it to stand in the refrigerator for about 10 minutes.

5 Bring plenty of salted water to the boil in a saucepan. With damp hands, shape the dough into eight small dumplings. Add the dumplings to the boiling water. Simmer, uncovered, over low heat for about 10 minutes.

6 Wash the chives, shake dry and cut into tiny pieces. Heat the beef broth. Transfer the dumplings to individual soup plates. Pour over the hot broth and sprinkle with finely cut chives.

Speckknödelsuppe
Clear soup with bread and bacon dumplings

Serves 4

2 day-old bread rolls
1 small onion
15 g flat-leaf parsley
100 g rindless, smoked streaky bacon
1 egg
about 6 tbsp milk
about 1 tbsp flour
15 g softened butter
1 tsp dried marjoram
salt
1 litre beef broth (see page 23)
1 bunch chives

Preparation time: 40 minutes (plus 30 minutes' standing time)

1,300 kJ/310 calories per portion

1 Cut the bread rolls into 1 cm cubes and place in a bowl. Peel and finely chop the onion. Wash the parsley, shake dry, remove the stalks and finely chop the leaves.

2 Dice the bacon and fry in a pan until the fat runs. Add the onion and fry until it is transparent, then add the onion and bacon to the bread. Whisk the egg in the milk and pour over the bread mixture. Add the flour, butter, parsley, marjoram and salt. Stir all the ingredients, then press the dough firmly together. Leave to stand for about 30 minutes.

3 Bring plenty of salted water to the boil in a large saucepan.

4 With damp hands, shape the dough into four dumplings. If the dough is too firm, add a little milk. If it is too soft, add some more flour.

5 Add the dumplings to the boiling water. Simmer, uncovered, over low heat for about 12 minutes. Meanwhile, heat the beef broth.

6 Add the dumplings to the broth. Wash the chives, shake dry, cut into small pieces, then sprinkle them over the soup.

Gailtaler Kirchtagssuppe

Hearty meat and vegetable soup

Takes a little time · Carinthia

Serves 6

200 g shoulder of beef
200 g shoulder of lamb
2 chicken legs (about 200 g each)
300 g root vegetables (carrots,
celeriac and parsnips)
5 black peppercorns
1 tbsp dried basil
6 saffron threads
ground cinnamon
12.5 cl whipping cream
2 egg yolks
salt · freshly ground white pepper

Preparation time: 2 hours

1,200 kJ/290 calories per portion

1 Wash the beef, lamb and the chicken legs. Trim, wash and coarsely chop the root vegetables. Place the beef, lamb, vegetables and black peppercorns in a large saucepan and cover with about 1.5 litres cold water.

2 Slowly bring the water to the boil, cover the pan and simmer the meat over low heat for about 1 hour, skimming the scum from the surface from time to time. Add the chicken legs, basil, saffron and a little cinnamon and continue cooking for a further 30 minutes.

3 Whisk the cream and egg yolks together. Strain the soup through a sieve, discarding the vegetables. Stir the cream mixture into the soup.

4 Cut the beef and lamb into small dice. Skin and bone the chicken legs, and cut the meat into bite-sized pieces. Return all the meat to the soup.

5 Reheat the soup to just below boiling point. Do not allow it to boil. Season with salt and pepper, and serve immediately.

Klachelsuppe

Pork soup

Simple but time consuming · Styria

Serves 4

1.5 kg knuckle of pork, cut into
2 cm thick slices
salt
1 small celeriac
1 small leek
2 medium-sized carrots
2 bay leaves
5 black peppercorns
1 tbsp wine vinegar
1 tbsp flour
1 large garlic clove
1 tbsp chopped fresh marjoram
freshly ground black pepper
2 tbsp freshly grated horseradish

*Preparation time: 30 minutes
(plus 3 hours' cooking time)*

3,300 kJ/790 calories per portion

1 Wash the meat and bring to the boil in about 4 litres water with 1 tsp salt. During the first 30 minutes, skim off the scum as it accumulates on the surface.

2 Trim, wash and coarsely chop all the vegetables. After removing all the scum, add the vegetables to the meat. Add the bay leaves and peppercorns. Cover the pan and simmer over low heat for about 3 hours.

3 When the meat is tender, strain the soup through a large sieve into another saucepan. Put about 12.5 cl of the liquid in a bowl and mix with the vinegar and flour. Stir the mixture into the soup and return to the boil.

4 Remove the meat from the bones, cut into 2 cm dice and add to the soup. Peel and crush the garlic and stir it into the soup. Add the marjoram and season with salt and pepper. Serve sprinkled with the grated horseradish.

Note: Bay leaves are aromatic, evergreen leaves which can be used to flavour hearty soups, stews, game and vegetable dishes. They are also combined with other herbs, such as thyme and parsley, to make a *bouquet garni*. Bay leaves can be used fresh or dried, but are removed from the dish before serving as the whole leaves are inedible. Bay leaves are also available ground.

Kürbiscremesuppe

Fairly easy • Styria   Cream of pumpkin soup   *Serves 4*

1 small pumpkin (about 700 g)
1 small onion
45 g butter
½ litre beef broth (see page 23; or use stock cubes)
salt
freshly ground white pepper
½ tsp ground caraway seeds
1 garlic clove
15 g dill
1 tbsp dried pumpkin seeds
12.5 cl whipping cream
a few drops of pumpkin seed oil (see below)

Preparation time: 40 minutes

1,200 kJ/290 calories per portion

1 Cut the pumpkin into quarters, and scoop out the seeds with a spoon. Cut the flesh into small dice. Peel and finely chop the onion.

2 Heat 30 g butter in a saucepan and fry the onion until transparent. Add the pumpkin and briefly fry with the onion before adding the beef broth. Season to taste with salt, pepper and the ground caraway seeds.

3 Peel and crush the garlic and add it to the soup. Simmer over low heat for about 15 minutes, until the pumpkin is soft.

4 Wash the dill, shake dry, remove the stalks and tear off small sprays of leaves. Heat the remaining butter in a frying pan and briefly fry the dried pumpkin seeds. Season lightly with salt.

5 Purée the pumpkin soup in a food processor or blender, adding the cream.

6 Drizzle the pumpkin seed oil over the soup, stirring to create a pattern on the surface. Sprinkle with the toasted pumpkin seeds and dill.

Pumpkins and pumpkin seed oil

Pumpkins, which can weigh anything up to 50 kg, are commonly grown in North America and Europe; about 90 per cent of Austria's crop comes from southern Styria. The firm, sweetish flesh—which contains a large amount of water—is high in protein, vitamins and minerals. Popular as a sweet pie filling, it can be boiled, roasted or puréed and is a delicious ingredient in soups and meat stews.

Pumpkin seed oil is derived from the vegetable's almond-shaped seeds—as much as 2.5 kg of seeds are needed to produce 1 litre of the protein-rich, dark-green oil. Its mild, spicy, nutty taste is particularly good with hearty, strong-flavoured salads and beef or sausage dishes, and it can also be used to flavour sauces. Stored in a well-sealed bottle, in a cool, dark place, it will keep for up to nine months.

Pumpkin seed oil is not very widely available in the UK; if you are unable to find it, you can use a nut oil, such as walnut oil, instead.

Wiensuppe mit Zimtkrusteln

Quick to prepare • Tyrol

Wine soup with cinnamon croûtons

Serves 4

4 slices day-old white bread
50 g butter
½ tsp ground cinnamon
¾ litre beef broth (see page 23; or use stock cubes)
¼ litre dry white wine
4 egg yolks
25 cl whipping cream
salt
freshly ground white pepper
sugar

Preparation time: 20 minutes

1,800 kJ/430 calories per portion

1 Remove the crusts from the bread, then cut into ½ cm dice. Heat the butter in a frying pan. Fry the bread dice in the butter, stirring constantly. Sprinkle with cinnamon, drain on paper towels and keep warm.

2 Mix the beef broth and the wine and bring to the boil. Whisk together the egg yolks and the cream.

3 Remove the soup from the heat. Use a hand whisk to mix the egg mixture into the soup. Reheat the soup to just below boiling point, stirring constantly. Do not allow it to boil. Season with salt, pepper and a little sugar.

4 Sprinkle the cinnamon croûtons over the soup just before serving.

Variation:
Biersuppe (Beer soup)
Substitute beer for the wine in this recipe. Add a little grated lemon rind to the seasoning, and omit the cinnamon.

Waldviertler Rahmsuppe

Beef broth with soured cream and caraway seeds

Serves 4

50 g rindless, smoked streaky bacon
1 small onion
30 g butter
¾ litre beef or vegetable broth (see page 23; or use stock cubes)
2 tbsp white wine vinegar
40 cl soured cream
2 tbsp flour
100 g black or wholemeal bread
1 small garlic clove
1 tsp caraway seeds
salt
freshly ground white pepper

Preparation time: 30 minutes

1,300 kJ/310 calories per portion

1 Chop the bacon into very small dice. Peel and finely chop the onion. Heat 15 g butter in a saucepan. Fry the bacon and onion until the onion is transparent.

2 Add the beef or vegetable broth and the wine vinegar and bring to the boil. Mix the soured cream and flour, stir into the broth, then simmer over low heat for about 10 minutes.

3 Meanwhile, cut the bread into ½ cm dice. Peel and finely chop the garlic. Heat the remaining butter in a frying pan and fry the garlic. Add the bread cubes and stir-fry them briefly over medium heat.

4 Season the soup with the caraway seeds, salt and pepper. Sprinkle with the croûtons just before serving.

Variation: Instead of croûtons, peel 2 medium-sized boiled potatoes while still warm, cut them into small dice and add to the soup just before serving.

Wiener Erdäpfelsuppe

Simple • Many regions

Potato and mushroom soup

Serves 4

1 medium-sized carrot
½ small celeriac
1 medium-sized onion
15 g butter
1 garlic clove
¾ litre beef broth (see page 23; or use stock cubes)
500 g floury potatoes
½ tsp dried marjoram
1 bay leaf
200 g ceps or button mushrooms
4 tbsp soured cream
freshly ground white pepper
salt
15 g flat-leaf parsley

Preparation time: 50 minutes

810 kJ/190 calories per portion

1 Trim and wash the carrot and celeriac. Thinly slice the carrot and finely dice the celeriac. Peel and finely chop the onion.

2 Heat the butter in a large saucepan and fry the onion until transparent. Peel and crush the garlic and add it to the pan. Add the diced vegetables and fry until lightly browned, stirring constantly. Add the beef broth, and bring to the boil.

3 Peel and wash the potatoes, then cut into small, even-sized dice. Add the diced potatoes, marjoram and bay leaf to the soup, cover the saucepan and cook over low heat for about 20 minutes.

4 Meanwhile, clean and thinly slice the ceps or button mushrooms. Add them to the soup 10 minutes before the end of the cooking time.

5 When the potatoes are done, remove the soup from the heat and discard the bay leaf. Stir in the soured cream and season with pepper and, if necessary, salt.

6 Wash the parsley, shake dry, remove the stalks and finely chop the leaves. Sprinkle them over the soup.

Ceps

The best-known and most popular of the wild mushrooms, ceps—known in Italy as *porcini*, or "little pigs"—are found all over Europe, flourishing between May and October in both deciduous and coniferous woodlands. They usually grow singly, but can appear in clusters of two or three. It is still not possible to cultivate ceps, a fact that makes them even more appealing to gourmets. They have a round brown cap and thick white stem that widens at the base. The nutritious, off-white flesh, which is firm and does not discolour, has a pleasant smell and rich, nutty flavour that makes them one of the tastiest mushrooms.

Widely available in supermarkets, ceps are delicious in soups, mixed with scrambled egg, gently simmered in a red wine sauce, or sautéed in butter with shallots and a hint of garlic. Ceps can also be bought dried, and make a quick, convenient addition to soups, salads and meat dishes.

STARTERS AND SNACKS

S tarters and little snacks, such as those that feature here, are a comparatively recent addition to Austrian cuisine, only gaining a place on the menu this century. Today, they are regarded as an integral part of a meal—though of quite secondary importance to the main course and the dessert, which are the focal points of traditional Austrian cooking.

Any starter, as the prologue to the meal, should help to stimulate the appetite, and arouse curiosity about the courses to follow; it should also harmonize in flavour and appearance with the dishes that are to come. In Austria, delicately flavoured vegetables such as asparagus and mushrooms—the latter an important ingredient in Auistrian cooking—are popular, and feature in such dishes as *Spargel mit Butterbröseln* and *Gebackene Champignons*. For more unusual starters, there are calf's sweetbreads and kidneys, *Kavaliersbries*, or calf's brains with scrambled egg, *Hirn mit Ei*.

The majority of the dishes in this chapter can also be served as in-between courses on more elaborate menus. Some, such as the little savoury croissants, *Schinkenkipferln*, are an excellent snack at any time of the day. Served, Austrian-style, with a fresh green salad, they make a delicious light supper.

Überbackener Karfiol

Cauliflower cheese

1 small cauliflower (about 600 g)
salt
15 g butter
4 tbsp fresh breadcrumbs
2 tbsp flour
12.5 cl home-made vegetable stock
(or use a stock cube) (optional)
1 egg yolk
12.5 cl whipping cream
2 tbsp freshly grated Parmesan or
Emmenthal cheese
freshly grated nutmeg
freshly ground white pepper
30 g butter, straight from the
refrigerator

Preparation time: 1 hour
(plus 15 minutes' standing time)

1,300 kJ/310 calories per portion

1 Cut off the tough main stalk and green outer leaves of the cauliflower, then soak the cauliflower in cold salted water for about 15 minutes.

2 Divide the cauliflower into florets, cutting the larger ones into small pieces (*above*), then trim and wash thoroughly.

3 Place the cauliflower in a saucepan, sprinkle with a little salt, then add just enough cold water to cover. Bring to the boil, cover the pan and cook over medium heat for about 12 minutes, until tender but still crisp.

4 Preheat the oven to 200°C (400°F or Mark 6). Butter four individual dishes or one large baking dish and sprinkle with half the breadcrumbs.

5 Drain the cooked cauliflower through a colander. Reserve about 12.5 cl of the cooking water, if you wish to use it for the sauce, and keep it warm until you are ready to make the sauce.

6 Gently heat the butter in a saucepan. Stir in the flour and cook until golden. Heat the vegetable stock, if using. Gradually stir the hot cauliflower water, or vegetable stock, if using, into the flour and butter and bring to the boil. Remove the pan from the heat and leave the sauce to cool slightly.

7 In a cup, whisk the egg yolk with the cream, then stir it into the sauce. Add the grated cheese. Season to taste with nutmeg, a little pepper and, if necessary, salt.

8 Place the cauliflower in the four individual dishes or large baking dish. Pour over the sauce and sprinkle with the remaining breadcrumbs. Cut the cold butter into slivers and dot it over the surface. Bake in the top of the oven for 20 minutes, until golden-brown.

Wine: Choose a dry white wine, such as one from the Burgenland region, to accompany this dish.

Variation:
Karfiol in Backteig
(Cauliflower in batter)
Cook the cauliflower as described above. Marinate the cooked cauliflower florets in the juice of 1 lemon, a little salt and 1 tbsp chopped fresh parsley. Mix 120 g flour, 1 egg yolk, 12.5 cl white wine or beer, a little salt, a few drops of oil and 12.5 cl milk to make a smooth batter. Fold in 1 stiffly beaten egg white and leave to stand for a few minutes. Dip the cauliflower florets in the batter, then deep-fry in hot oil. Drain thoroughly before serving.

Spargel mit Butterbröseln

Simple but elegant · Marchfeld **Asparagus with toasted breadcrumbs** *Serves 4*

1 kg white asparagus
1 tsp salt
1 tsp sugar
1 tsp lemon juice
5 g butter
finely chopped flat-leaf parsley
for garnish

For the toasted breadcrumbs:
100 g butter
80 g fresh breadcrumbs
salt

Preparation time: 30 minutes

1,300 kJ/310 calories per portion

1 Wash the asparagus thoroughly, then lay the spears on a work surface and carefully peel them, working from tip to base. The easiest way to do this is with a potato peeler. Cut off and discard the woody ends. Divide the asparagus spears into three bundles and bind them at the top and bottom with kitchen twine.

2 Pour about 2 litres water into a saucepan. Add the 1 tsp salt, sugar, lemon juice and the 5 g butter. Bring to the boil. Carefully slide the asparagus bundles into the boiling water, cover the pan and simmer over low heat for about 15 minutes, until the asparagus is tender but still crisp. It is cooked when it can be easily pierced with a fork.

3 Meanwhile, heat the 100 g butter in a frying pan and fry the breadcrumbs over medium heat until golden-brown. Season lightly with salt.

4 Lift the asparagus out of the water, drain thoroughly and remove the twine. Arrange the asparagus on a serving dish, sprinkle with the breadcrumbs and garnish with the chopped parsley.

Asparagus

The sturdy, succulent shoots of the asparagus plant, a member of the lily family, are regarded as the most exquisite of vegetables. There are several species of asparagus, which is cultivated extensively throughout Europe and the United States. In the Marchfeld region of Lower Austria, white asparagus is harvested from mid-May until the end of June. The shoots, or "spears", are cut as soon as the heads begin to poke through the soil, so they remain colourless. The thinner, green asparagus, which grows above ground (hence its colour), comes principally from France and Italy; this variety is more popular in Britain and America.

You can tell if asparagus is fresh by its light colour and the smooth texture of the cut ends. Fresh spears also have a ringing sound when rubbed together. Asparagus is best eaten immediately; if you are keeping it for more than a day before using, wrap the spears in a slightly damp cloth and refrigerate.

White asparagus has a thick, woody skin that must be peeled before cooking. With green asparagus, peel just the ends of thicker stems.

Kavaliersbries

Calf's sweetbreads with mushrooms

Takes time • Many regions

Serves 4

2 calf's sweetbreads (about 600 g—
you may need to order them in
advance from your butcher)
salt
1 tbsp white wine vinegar
250 g mushrooms
2 tbsp flour
30 g butter
12.5 cl veal or beef stock
(see page 23)
30 g flat-leaf parsley
12.5 cl whipping cream
freshly ground white pepper

*Preparation time: 1 hour
(plus 2 hours' soaking time)*

1,400 kJ/330 calories per portion

1 Soak the sweetbreads in water for about 2 hours, changing the water several times, until all the blood has run out and they are completely white.

2 Transfer the sweetbreads to a saucepan and add enough cold water to cover. Season with a little salt and the vinegar. Bring to the boil and simmer, uncovered, over low heat for about 15 minutes. Meanwhile, clean and thinly slice the mushrooms.

3 Rinse the sweetbreads in cold water, discarding the skin and blood vessels. Slice and coat in the flour.

4 Heat the butter in a frying pan and stir-fry the sliced sweetbreads over

low heat until they are golden-brown on both sides.

5 Heat the veal or beef stock. Pour it over the sweetbreads and add the mushrooms. Cover the pan and cook over low heat for about 15 minutes, until the sweetbreads are tender.

6 Wash the parsley, shake dry, remove the stalks and chop the leaves.

7 Stir the cream into the sweetbreads. Season to taste with salt and pepper. Serve sprinkled with chopped parsley, accompanied by freshly baked bread.

Wine: A light, dry white wine goes well with this dish.

Gebackene Champignons

Mushrooms fried in breadcrumbs

Quick and easy • Many regions

Serves 4

500 g mushrooms
2 eggs
80 g plain flour
100 g fresh breadcrumbs
salt
coconut (see Note), or vegetable, oil
for deep-frying
1 unwaxed lemon
30 g parsley

Preparation time: 30 minutes

2,000 kJ/480 calories per portion

1 Trim the mushrooms, rinse briefly under cold running water and pat dry. Cut the larger mushrooms in half. Whisk the eggs on a plate with a fork. Put the flour and breadcrumbs on separate plates.

2 Season the mushrooms with salt and coat with flour, shaking off any excess. Dip them in the beaten egg, drain off the surplus egg, then coat in the breadcrumbs. Shake the mushrooms thoroughly to remove any loose breadcrumbs, otherwise they will burn.

3 Heat a generous amount of oil in a large frying pan and fry the mushrooms over medium heat for about 5 minutes,

until golden. Remove them from the pan and drain on paper towels.

4 Wash the lemon in hot water, pat dry and cut into four wedges. Wash the parsley, shake and divide into sprigs.

5 Arrange the mushrooms on a warmed serving dish and garnish with the lemon wedges and parsley sprigs.

Note: Coconut oil is dense, white and buttery, more fat-like than oily. It is widely used in Southeast Asian and Indian cookery, imparting a coconut flavour to food that is cooked in it. Unusually for a vegetable oil, it is very high in saturated fat.

Hirn mit Ei

Not difficult • Substantial

Calf's brains with scrambled egg

Serves 4

500 g calf's brains
1 small onion
30 g flat-leaf parsley
30 g butter
4 eggs
salt
freshly ground white pepper

Preparation time: 25 minutes
(plus 30 minutes' soaking time)

1,500 kJ/360 calories per portion

1 Soak the brains in cold water for about 30 minutes. Remove the skin, blood vessels and large veins, then finely chop the brains. Peel and finely chop the onion. Wash the parsley, shake dry, remove the stalks and finely chop the leaves.

2 Heat the butter in a frying pan and fry the onion until transparent. Add the brains and chopped parsley and fry over medium heat for about 5 minutes, stirring occasionally.

3 Whisk the eggs thoroughly. Pour the beaten egg over the brains in the frying pan and cook briefly, until the egg begins to set.

4 Season with salt and pepper, then serve immediately, accompanied by a green salad.

Wine: A light, dry white wine is an ideal choice to serve with this dish.

 # Saure Nierndln

Takes a little time • Vorarlberg **Calf's kidneys with soured cream** *Serves 4*

2 calf's kidneys (about 500 g)
2 tbsp flour
15 g flat-leaf parsley
1 small onion
30 g butter
1 tbsp white wine vinegar
12.5 cl beef broth (see page 23; or use a stock cube)
4 tbsp soured cream
salt
freshly ground white pepper

Preparation time: 30 minutes (plus 30 minutes' soaking time)

1,100 kJ/260 calories per portion

1 Cut the kidneys in half and remove all the skin and tubes. Soak them in cold water for about 30 minutes, changing the water several times.

2 Pat the kidneys dry, then cut into 1 cm-thick slices and coat in the flour.

3 Wash the parsley, shake dry, remove the stalks and finely chop the leaves. Peel and finely chop the onion. Heat the butter in a frying pan and fry the onion until transparent. Add the sliced kidneys and stir-fry over medium heat for about 5 minutes.

4 Add the vinegar and then the beef broth. Bring to the boil, then remove from the heat. Stir in the soured cream and season with salt and pepper.

5 Serve, accompanied, if you like, by puréed potato sprinkled with parsley.

Note: The characteristic flavour and grainy texture of vitamin-rich kidneys is a great favourite with gourmets. The best kidneys come from a young animal, preferably a calf or a lamb. As with all offal, kidneys should be bought and cooked on the same day, and cleaned thoroughly before use. Only add salt after they are cooked, otherwise they will be tough.

Schinkenkipferln
Croissants with ham filling

Serves 4

For the dough:
150 g boiled floury potatoes,
cooked the day before
125 g quark
120 g flour
50 g butter
1 egg
freshly grated nutmeg
salt

For the filling and topping:
200 g sliced, lean smoked ham
a few parsley sprigs
15 g butter
1 tbsp flour
freshly ground black pepper
1 tsp dried marjoram
1 egg yolk
1 tbsp caraway seeds

Preparation time: 1½ hours

1,700 kJ/400 calories per portion

1 To make the dough, peel the potatoes, then grate or mash. Rub the quark through a sieve and add to the potato. Add the flour, butter and egg. Season with a little nutmeg and salt.

2 Quickly knead all the ingredients to make a fairly smooth dough. Cover and leave to stand in the refrigerator for about 30 minutes.

3 Meanwhile, make the filling. Finely chop the ham. Wash the parsley, shake dry, remove the stalks and finely chop the leaves. Heat the butter in a frying pan and stir-fry the ham until lightly browned. Sprinkle the flour into the pan and allow to brown. Season with pepper and the marjoram. Stir in the parsley. Mix thoroughly until smooth, adding 1 tbsp water, if necessary. Leave to cool.

4 Preheat the oven to 220°C (425°F or Mark 7). Whisk the egg yolk in a cup with 1 tbsp cold water. Line a baking sheet with greaseproof paper.

5 On a floured surface, roll out the dough to a thickness of about ½ cm.

Cut the dough into four squares and cut each square in half diagonally, to make eight triangles. Place a walnut-sized piece of filling in the centre of each triangle (*above*).

6 Starting at the long edge, roll up the pastry triangles, to make small bulbous rolls that have pointed ends (*above*). Shape the rolls into

croissants and place on the baking sheet, with the join downwards. Brush with egg yolk and sprinkle with the caraway seeds.

7 Bake in the centre of the oven for 25 minutes, until golden-brown, and serve while still warm.

Wine: Choose a dry white wine or cold beer to accompany this dish.

Note: Caraway seeds are widely used in Austrian cooking, in both sweet and savoury dishes; their distinctive aromatic taste derives from a high essential oil content. To retain the flavour for as long as possible, caraway seeds should be stored in a dark place in a well-sealed contained.

If you use non-floury potatoes for this recipe and find that the dough is too sticky, add another 30 to 40 g flour.

Rindfleischsalat mit Kernöl

Beef salad with eggs and peppers

400 g lean, cooked beef
2 tbsp wine vinegar
3 tbsp pumpkin seed oil (see page 30)
salt
freshly ground black pepper
1 small pickled gherkin
1 tbsp capers
2 eggs
1 small onion
1 small sweet green pepper
1 small sweet red pepper
1 bunch chives

Preparation time: 30 minutes

1,110 kJ/260 calories per portion

1 Slice the cooked beef very thinly.

2 To make the dressing, mix the vinegar, oil, salt and pepper. Chop the gherkin and capers very finely, then stir them into the dressing. Drizzle the dressing over the meat and leave to marinate for about 15 minutes.

3 Boil the eggs for about 10 minutes until hard. Rinse in cold water, shell and slice thinly.

4 Peel the onion and slice into thin rings. Wash the peppers, cut them in half crosswise, remove the stalks, seeds and ribs, then cut the flesh into thin rings.

5 Transfer the marinated meat to four individual plates and arrange the sliced eggs, peppers and onion rings on top. Wash the chives, shake dry and cut into tiny pieces.

6 Sprinkle the salad with the finely cut chives and serve with crusty bread.

Drink: Cold beer or cider is a good accompaniment to this dish.

Variations: Instead of beef, substitute smoked sausage, tongue or cooked ham.

Steirischer Röhrlsalat

Dandelion salad with egg and tomato

2 eggs
400 g fresh young dandelion leaves (see Note)
2 tbsp white wine vinegar
3 tbsp pumpkin seed oil (see page 30)
dried tarragon
1 tsp dry mustard, mixed with a little water
salt • freshly ground black pepper
1 small onion
30 g parsley
2 small tomatoes

Preparation time: 30 minutes

780 kJ/190 calories per portion

1 Boil the eggs for about 10 minutes until hard, then leave to cool.

2 Sort the dandelion leaves, discarding the tough stalks. Wash the leaves thoroughly, dry and tear into small pieces. Arrange in a salad bowl.

3 Whisk the vinegar, oil, tarragon, mustard, salt and pepper in a bowl. Peel and finely chop the onion, then stir it into the dressing. Wash the parsley, shake dry, remove the stalks and finely chop the leaves. Add to the dressing.

4 Shell the eggs. Finely chop the whites and mash the yolks with a fork. Stir the yolks into the dressing and leave to stand.

5 Sprinkle the dandelion leaves with the chopped egg whites. Pour the dressing over the leaves and allow to marinate for about 5 minutes. Wash the tomatoes, cut each one into eight wedges and use to garnish the salad. Serve the salad with crusty brown bread.

Note: Dandelion leaves are an excellent "free food", rich in vitamins and minerals. In Austria and other European countries, dandelions are cultivated and these varieties have a milder, more subtle flavour than the wild ones. If preferred, use a mixture of dandelions and other salad leaves for this salad.

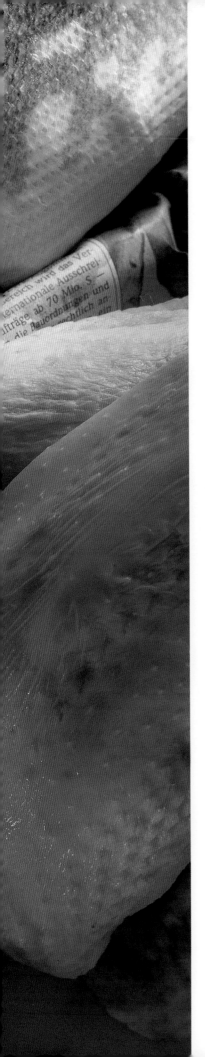

MEAT, FISH AND POULTRY

The Austrians are renowned for their love of meat, which is reflected in the wealth and variety of their recipes—from quick, pan-fried dishes such as *Butterschnitzel*, and succulent roasts, to cheaper cuts of meat, cooked gently and slowly to tenderize them. A favourite meat is veal—the principal ingredient in the famous Viennese *Wiener Schnitzel*—but there are also many delicious ways of cooking beef and pork. Yet another celebrated Viennese speciality is boiled beef (*Tafelspitz*); during the early part of the century, the city had restaurants that offered as many as 24 different varieties!

Poultry, too, has always been popular, with many dishes still being prepared in the traditional manner: for example, the breaded fried chicken dish, *Wiener Backhendl*, one of the classics of Austrian cuisine, is made in the same way today as it was in the eighteenth century. For dinner parties and festive occasions, stuffed goose, *Gefüllte Gans*, is a firm favourite.

Although Austria has no coastline, it is well watered, and its many lakes, rivers and mountain streams are generously stocked with freshwater fish such as carp and pike. The fish dishes in this chapter are all substantial enough to be served as a main course.

Wiener Tafelspitz

Boiled beef

1 kg soup bones

salt

2.5 kg rolled brisket

1 Hamburg parsley root (see Note), or parsnip

1 medium-sized carrot

½ small celeriac

½ leek

2 garlic cloves

1 medium-sized onion

1 tsp black peppercorns

1 large bunch chives

freshly grated nutmeg

Preparation time: 30 minutes (plus 3½ hours' cooking time)

1,600 kJ/380 calories per portion

1 Place the soup bones in a large saucepan and cover with water. Bring to the boil, allow to boil briefly, then strain through a sieve. Discard the water. Wash the bones thoroughly and remove any splinters. Return the bones to the saucepan and add 3 litres cold water and 1 tsp salt. Bring to the boil.

2 Rinse the brisket under cold running water. Add it to the bones in the saucepan as soon as the water comes to the boil. Return to the boil, then simmer over very low heat for 30 minutes, skimming off the scum as it forms on the surface.

3 Meanwhile, trim the root vegetables and leek, wash thoroughly and cut into chunks. Peel the garlic cloves.

4 Remove the loose, outer skin and the root from the onion, then wash the onion and cut it in half crosswise. Take one onion half and dry-fry it in a frying pan until the cut surface is well browned.

5 When all the scum has been removed from the liquid, add the root vegetables, leek, garlic, the remaining onion half and the peppercorns to the meat. Simmer gently, uncovered, for 3 hours, until the meat is cooked and can easily be pierced with a fork.

6 Wash the chives, shake dry and cut into tiny pieces.

7 Remove the cooked meat from the stock, then strain through a fine sieve. Discard the vegetables. Skim off some

of the fat from the surface. Season with a little nutmeg and salt.

8 Carve the beef across the grain into thick slices and arrange on a warmed serving dish. Season lightly with salt. Drizzle 2 tbsp of the hot stock per portion over the meat, then sprinkle with the finely cut chives. (You can use the rest of the stock for making soup or gravy.) The classic accompaniments to serve with *Tafelspitz* are apple and horseradish sauce, chive sauce (see right) and sauté potatoes.

Wine: A robust, full-bodied red wine, such as one from Burgenland, goes well with this classic dish.

Accompaniments:

Apple and horseradish sauce

Peel and finely grate 2 medium-sized, tart eating apples. Immediately stir into it 2 tbsp wine vinegar. Add 1 tbsp sugar, 2 tbsp freshly grated horseradish and a little salt. Mix thoroughly.

Chive sauce

Moisten 2 day-old bread rolls with 5 tbsp clear beef stock or water and place them in a blender or food processor. Add 2 hard-boiled egg yolks, 2 tbsp wine vinegar, 12.5 cl vegetable oil, white pepper and salt and beat to a thick sauce. Wash a large

bunch of chives and cut them into tiny pieces. Stir about two thirds of the chives into the sauce and sprinkle the rest on top.

Note: Long, slow cooking is particularly suitable for brisket as it breaks down the tough fibres, ensuring tender meat.

Hamburg parsley root is a popular ingredient in eastern and northern European cooking. Resembling a small, even-shaped parsnip, it tastes like a combination of parsnip, parsley and celery. Hamburg parsley root is available all year round, but can be difficult to find in the UK; if you are unable to buy it, use parsnip instead.

Zwiebelrostbraten

Beef escalopes with onion rings

2 medium-sized onions
2 tbsp flour
4 fillet steaks (about 180 g each)
salt
freshly ground black pepper
2 tbsp vegetable oil
45 g butter
12.5 cl beef stock (see page 23; or use stock cubes)

Preparation time: 30 minutes

2,300 kJ/550 calories per portion

1 Peel the onions and cut them into thin rings. Put the flour on a flat plate.

2 Rinse the steaks under cold running water, pat dry and press them flat, using the ball of your thumb. Make several cuts in the fat around the edge, to prevent it curling up while frying.

3 Season both sides of the steaks with salt and pepper, then coat with flour on one side only. Heat the oil in a large frying pan.

4 Place the steaks, floured side downwards, in the hot oil. Fry for about 4 minutes over medium heat, then turn over and fry for a further 4 minutes. The steaks should still be slightly pink in the middle.

5 While the steaks are cooking, heat 30 g butter in a second frying pan. Add the onion rings and fry until crisp and golden. Drain off any surplus butter, season the onions with salt, and keep warm.

6 Arrange the cooked steaks on a warmed serving dish and keep warm. Add the beef stock to the meat juices in the pan and bring to the boil. Stir in the remaining butter, then pour the sauce over the meat. Arrange the onion rings on top of the steaks.

Wine: A full-bodied red wine, such as one from Burgenland, is an excellent choice to accompany this dish.

Onions

Onions have been cultivated all over the world for more than 5,000 years. Indispensable in any kitchen as a vital flavouring ingredient, they are also valued for their medicinal qualities, aiding digestion, and stimulating the appetite.

The most common cooking onions are globe (yellow) onions, notably the large, mild, Spanish onion. Dark, purple-red onions, which have a sweet flavour, are delicious raw and, cut into thin rings, are a striking salad ingredient. They retain some of their purple colour when cooked.

Another attractive onion is the

mild and sweet white onion. Small bulb onions, such as pearl onions, are good for pickling, and can be added to stews and casseroles. Shallots, with two or more "cloves" resembling a bulb of

garlic, have a distinctive mild flavour that is an essential ingredient in classic French cuisine. Spring onions are popular in Oriental cookery, in stir fries and added to salads.

Wiener Schnitzel

Veal escalopes fried in breadcrumbs

Simple but elegant • Many regions

Serves 4

4 veal escalopes (about 5 mm thick and 180 g each)
salt
2 eggs
100 g flour
150 g fresh breadcrumbs
250 g pork dripping, or
25 cl vegetable oil
1 unwaxed lemon

Preparation time: 40 minutes

3,200 kJ/760 calories per portion

1 Rinse the escalopes under cold running water, pat dry and then beat lightly to flatten them. Season lightly with salt.

2 Whisk the eggs on a soup plate. Put the flour and the breadcrumbs onto separate plates.

3 Coat the escalopes in flour, shaking off any excess, then dip them in the beaten egg. Drain off the excess egg and coat in breadcrumbs.

4 Heat the dripping or oil in a large frying pan until the fat is hot enough to hiss when a wet fork is dipped in it. Arrange the escalopes in the pan, keeping them apart from one another and away from the edge of the pan (fry one or two at a time, if necessary). Fry over high heat for about 4 minutes on each side, until golden, taking care not to pierce the meat as it is turned. Shake the pan frequently while cooking to prevent the meat sticking to the pan and burning.

5 Wash the lemon in hot water, pat dry and cut lengthwise into four wedges.

6 Drain the cooked escalopes on paper towels and arrange on a warmed serving dish with the lemon wedges. Serve with a potato or cucumber salad.

Wine: Serve a fresh, dry white wine with this classic Viennese dish.

Kalbsgulasch

Veal and onion goulash

Easy but takes time • Winter dish

Serves 4

700 g shoulder of veal
300 g onions
2 tbsp pork dripping, or vegetable oil
2 tbsp sweet paprika
1 tbsp wine vinegar
about ¾ litre beef stock (see page 23; or use stock cubes)
grated rind of ½ unwaxed lemon
salt
1 garlic clove
1 tbsp tomato purée

Preparation time: 1¼ hours

1,300 kJ/310 calories per portion

1 Rinse the meat, pat dry and cut into 3 cm cubes. Cut the cubes in half.

2 Peel the onions and slice them into thin rings. Heat the dripping or oil in a fire proof casserole and stir-fry the onions over medium heat until golden. Sprinkle the paprika over the onions, then immediately add the vinegar and about 3 tbsp beef stock. Add the meat and season with the grated lemon rind and a little salt. Peel and crush the garlic and add it to the casserole.

3 Cover the casserole and braise over low heat for about 35 minutes. Stir from time to time, adding a little more beef stock each time, if necessary, to prevent it drying out.

4 Add just enough beef stock to cover the meat. Stir in the tomato purée and simmer for a further 5 minutes, then season to taste with salt. Serve with dumplings.

Drink: A glass of beer is the best accompaniment to this hearty stew.

Gefüllte Kalbsbrust

Takes time • Special occasions

Breast of veal with mushroom stuffing

Serves 4

1 kg boned breast of veal
salt
freshly ground black pepper
2 bread rolls
12.5 cl milk
250 g mushrooms
30 g flat-leaf parsley
1 small onion
30 g butter
2 eggs
freshly grated nutmeg
3 tbsp clarified butter (see
Glossary), or vegetable oil
2 tbsp crème fraîche

**Preparation time: 45 minutes
(plus 1¾ hours' cooking time)**

2,700 kJ/640 calories per portion

1 Rinse the meat and pat dry. With a sharp knife, cut a deep slit in the meat (*above*) for the stuffing. Rub inside and out with salt and pepper.

2 Soak the bread rolls in the milk. Clean and thinly slice the mushrooms. Wash the parsley and shake dry. Reserve a few leaves for garnishing and finely chop the remainder. Peel and finely chop the onion.

3 Heat the butter in a frying pan and fry the onion until transparent. Add the mushrooms and parsley and fry for a further 5 minutes. Leave to cool.

4 Squeeze the moisture out of the bread rolls. Stir the bread into the mushroom mixture with the eggs. Season with salt, pepper and nutmeg.

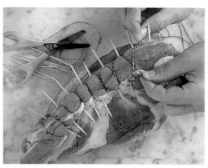

5 Preheat the oven to 200°C (400°F or Mark 6). Fill the breast of veal with the stuffing, packing it loosely, to allow room for it to expand while cooking.

Secure the opening with toothpicks, then bind with kitchen twine in a criss-cross pattern.

6 Heat the clarified butter or oil in a roasting pan and brown the stuffed meat on all sides.

7 Lay the joint in the pan, smooth side downwards, and place in the centre of the oven. Cook the meat for 30 minutes, then turn it over. Cook for a further 1¼ hours, until lightly browned, basting frequently with the pan juices.

8 Remove the meat from the pan and keep warm. Strain the pan juices through a fine metal sieve, and stir in the crème fraîche.

9 Remove the toothpicks and kitchen twine from the meat and carve it into slices. Garnish with the reserved parsley. Serve with the sauce, accompanied by fresh baby vegetables, or boiled rice.

Variation: Instead of mushrooms and parsley, use 350 g fresh spinach for the stuffing. Wash and trim the spinach. Place it in a saucepan with just the water that clings to the leaves and heat until it wilts. Leave to cool, squeeze out the moisture, chop finely and mix with the soaked bread rolls.

Butterschnitzel mit Püree

Easy • Family dish **Veal rissoles with puréed potatoes** *Serves 4*

800 g floury potatoes
1 tsp caraway seeds
salt
2 bread rolls
about 40 cl milk
500 g minced veal
2 eggs
freshly ground black pepper
¼ tsp freshly grated nutmeg
about 50 g fresh breadcrumbs
90 g butter
4 tbsp beef stock (see page 23; or use a stock cube)
1 medium-sized onion
2 tbsp vegetable oil

Preparation time: 1¼ hours

2,800 kJ/670 calories per portion

1 Peel and wash the potatoes, then cut them into medium-sized chunks. Place in a saucepan with ½ litre water, the caraway seeds and a little salt. Bring the water to the boil and simmer the potatoes over low heat for about 25 minutes, until very soft.

2 Soak the bread rolls in 12.5 cl milk. Rinse the meat and pat dry.

3 Squeeze the moisture out of the bread rolls, tear them into small pieces and add to the minced veal. Stir in the eggs and season with salt, pepper and a little nutmeg.

4 Knead the meat mixture thoroughly, adding enough breadcrumbs to make a soft but workable dough. Shape into eight balls, then press them into oval rissoles, the thickness of a finger.

5 Heat 30 g butter in a frying pan. Over low heat, fry the rissoles on each side for about 8 minutes, until golden-brown. Remove the rissoles from the pan and keep warm.

6 Pour the beef stock into the frying pan and bring to the boil. Reduce the heat and stir in 30 g butter. Keep the sauce warm.

7 Drain the potatoes and finely mash them. Bring ¼ litre milk to the boil with a little salt and nutmeg. Using a hand whisk, stir the milk into the mashed potatoes, a little at a time, to create a smooth purée. Add a little more milk, if necessary. Stir in the remaining butter.

8 Peel the onion and cut into thin rings. Heat the oil in a frying pan and fry the onion rings until golden-brown.

9 Transfer the rissoles and puréed potato to four warmed plates. Pour the sauce over the rissoles and arrange the onion rings on top of the potato. Serve with buttered peas.

Wine: Choose a spicy, flowery white wine, such as a Grüner Veltliner from the Wachau region on the south bank of the Danube.

Variations:
Instead of fried onion rings, top the potato purée with finely chopped fresh herbs (such as chives or parsley), sweet paprika, breadcrumbs sautéed in butter, or finely chopped crispy bacon. If you like, stir a little freshly grated horseradish or piquant cheese into the purée; to make it creamier (but higher in calories), replace the milk with cream, or a mixture of the two.

Salonbeuschel

Calf's lungs and heart in a soured cream sauce

Serves 4

800 g calf's lungs and heart
1 medium-sized onion
6 black peppercorns
1 medium-sized carrot
1 large Hamburg parsley root (see
Note, page 53), or parsnip
1 small leek
½ small celeriac
1 clove
1 bay leaf
1 sprig thyme
2 small pickled gherkins
30 g flat-leaf parsley
rind of ¼ unwaxed lemon
1 garlic clove
1 tsp capers
1 anchovy fillet
60 g butter
2 tbsp dry white wine
1 tbsp white wine vinegar
1 tbsp lemon juice
25 cl whipping cream
12.5 cl soured cream
1 tbsp mustard
dried marjoram
salt
freshly ground white pepper
marjoram leaves for garnish

Preparation time: 1 hour
(plus 1½ hours' cooking time)

2,500 kJ/600 calories per portion

1 Thoroughly wash the lungs and heart inside and out, removing any remaining blood, and cutting out large blood vessels. Peel the onion and cut in half. Reserve one half for the sauce. Crush the peppercorns. Trim the carrot, Hamburg parsley root or parsnip, leek and celeriac. Wash thoroughly and chop coarsely. Place all these ingredients in a large saucepan with 1 litre cold water.

2 Add the clove, bay leaf and thyme. Bring the water to the boil, cover the pan and cook over low heat for about 1½ hours.

3 Drain the liquid from the meat, reserving about ½ litre of stock. Strain the reserved stock through a sieve. Discard the vegetables. Rinse the meat under cold running water, then leave to cool. Remove any gristle and cut the meat into short, thin strips.

4 Finely chop the gherkins. Wash the parsley, shake dry and remove the coarse stalks. Wash the lemon rind in hot water. Peel the garlic. Finely chop the parsley, lemon rind, garlic, capers, anchovy fillet and the reserved onion half. Sauté all these ingredients in butter in a large frying pan.

5 Add the white wine, wine vinegar, lemon juice and reserved meat stock and cook for about 10 minutes. Add the meat strips and gherkins, then simmer for a further 10 minutes.

6 Gradually stir in the cream, soured cream, mustard and a little marjoram. Taste and season with salt and pepper, if necessary. Serve garnished with marjoram leaves, accompanied, if you like, by slices of dumpling (see below).

Suggested accompaniment:
Serviettenknödel
(Dumplings made in a tea towel)
Whisk 12.5 cl milk with 3 egg yolks in a large bowl. Cut 500 g bread, with the crusts removed, into small dice and add to the egg and milk mixture, pushing it into the mixture until covered. Add 30 g melted butter and season with salt, pepper and a little nutmeg. Beat 3 egg whites until stiff and fold into the mixture. Shape the dough into a roll about 8 cm in diameter. Grease a clean tea towel with butter and wrap the dough, tying the tea towel with kitchen twine at each end. Bring a large saucepan of water to the boil, add the dumpling and simmer for about 35 minutes. Leave to stand for a few minutes, then cut into slices.

Drink: Serve with cold beer.

Note: Marjoram is cultivated throughout central and southern Europe. The sweetly spiced leaves, which can be used fresh or dried, have a flavour similar to thyme, for which it can be substituted in cooking. Marjoram is excellent as a seasoning in meat and poultry dishes, soups and stews, stuffings and omelettes.

Schweinsbraten

Roast pork with potato dumplings

Serves 4

600 g floury potatoes
1 kg pork (preferably blade bone or loin)
salt
freshly ground black pepper
5 garlic cloves
3 tbsp pork dripping, or vegetable oil
1 tsp caraway seeds

Preparation time: 1 hour
(plus 1½ hours' cooking time)

2,600 kJ/620 calories per portion

1 To make the dumplings, boil 400 g potatoes in their skins. Peel and mash the potatoes while still hot. Spread out the mashed potato on a baking sheet and leave to cool and dry out for about 1 hour.

2 Rinse the meat under cold running water, pat dry and rub all over with plenty of salt and pepper. Peel the garlic cloves and cut into slivers. Cut small slits in the meat with the tip of a sharp knife and insert slivers of garlic into the slits.

3 Preheat the oven to 220°C (425°F or Mark 7). Heat the dripping or oil in a roasting pan on top of the stove, add the joint and brown on all sides over high heat.

4 Turn the joint fat side down in the pan and roast in the centre of the oven for about 45 minutes, basting with the pan juices about every 10 minutes. Turn the meat over and sprinkle with the caraway seeds, then cook for a further 45 minutes, until crisp and brown. If the meat starts to look dry, pour a very small amount of hot water into the pan beside the joint. The meat is done when the thickest part can easily be pierced with a fine skewer or a carving fork.

5 Meanwhile, peel the remaining raw potatoes. Wash, then grate them into a bowl of cold water. Using a slotted spoon, transfer the grated potatoes to a clean tea towel. Wrap in the tea towel and squeeze out as much liquid as possible, collecting the liquid in a bowl. Leave the liquid to stand until all the starch sinks to the bottom of the bowl, then carefully drain off the clear water. Knead the starch, raw and mashed potatoes and 1 tsp salt together to make a firm dough.

6 Bring plenty of salted water to the boil in a saucepan. Shape the potato dough into four dumplings. Place the potato dumplings in the boiling water and cook over medium heat for about 20 minutes, carefully turning the dumplings over half way through the cooking time.

7 Remove the cooked dumplings from the pan with a slotted spoon. Drain thoroughly and keep warm until you are ready to serve.

8 Loosely wrap the meat in aluminium foil. Turn off the oven and leave the meat to stand in the oven for about 10 minutes.

9 Meanwhile, add a little water to the juices in the roasting pan and bring to the boil. Strain through a fine metal sieve, and season with salt and pepper.

10 Carve the pork into thick slices and arrange on a warmed serving dish with the potato dumplings. Serve with the sauce.

Drink: Serve with a chilled lager or beer.

Schweinsjungfer im Schlafrock
Pork fillet in a puff pastry crust

Serves 4

400 g frozen puff pastry, thawed
1 medium-sized onion
300 g mushrooms
15 g flat-leaf parsley
30 g butter
salt
freshly ground black pepper
800 g pork fillet
2 tbsp clarified butter (see Glossary),
or vegetable oil
1 tsp dried rosemary
1 egg
4 thin slices cooked ham
(about 80 g)

Preparation time: 2¼ hours
(plus 50 minutes' standing time)

3,700 kJ/880 calories per portion

1 Peel and finely chop the onion. Clean and finely chop the mushrooms. Wash the parsley, shake dry, remove the stalks and finely chop the leaves.

2 Heat the butter in a frying pan and fry the chopped onion until transparent. Add the mushrooms and the parsley and stir-fry over high heat for about 5 minutes, until nearly all the liquid has evaporated. Leave the mushroom mixture to cool completely and then season generously with salt and pepper.

3 Rinse the pork fillet and pat dry, removing the skin and fat. Heat the clarified butter or oil in a roasting pan and cook the meat over high heat for about 20 minutes, until well browned all over. Leave to cool, then rub the meat on all sides with the rosemary and salt and pepper.

4 Separate the egg and whisk the white with 1 tsp water. On a lightly floured surface, roll out the pastry to a rectangle about 25 by 30 cm. Cover with aluminium foil and leave to stand for 20 minutes.

5 Cut off and reserve a strip from all round the edge of the pastry for use as decoration. Brush the edge of the pastry rectangle with egg white, to a width of about 1 cm. Arrange the sliced ham on top of the unbrushed pastry, then spread evenly with half the mushroom mixture.

6 Place the browned pork fillet in the centre (*above*) and cover it with the remaining mushroom mixture. Fold the pastry up over the meat and press the edges firmly together to seal in the meat.

7 Preheat the oven to 220°C (425° or Mark 7). Rinse a baking sheet with cold water. Lay the meat in its pastry case on the baking sheet, with the join downwards. Using a pastry wheel, cut the reserved pastry into fluted strips. Arrange the strips on top of the roll in a lattice pattern (*above*) and prick the pastry in several places with a fork. Whisk the egg yolk slightly, then brush the pastry with it. Leave to stand for about 20 minutes.

8 Bake in the centre of the oven for about 40 minutes, until golden-brown. Turn off the oven and open the door, then leave the meat to stand for about 10 minutes. Cut into thick slices and arrange on a warmed serving dish.

Wurzelkarpfen mit Kren

Simple but elegant • Styria **Carp fillet with horseradish** *Serves 4*

½ litre dry white wine
1 tbsp cider vinegar
5 black peppercorns
2 bay leaves
salt
1 medium-sized onion
600 g root vegetables (celeriac,
carrots, parsnip)
4 carp fillets (about 200 g each • see
Note)
2 tbsp freshly grated horseradish

Preparation time: 1 hour

1,600 kJ/380 calories per portion

1 Bring the wine, vinegar and 1 litre water to the boil in a saucepan. Add the peppercorns, bay leaves and 1 tsp salt. Meanwhile, peel and coarsely chop the onion. Trim and wash the root vegetables. Set aside half, and coarsely chop the reminder. Add them to the pan and simmer over low heat for about 20 minutes.

2 Add the carp fillets to the hot stock, cover the pan and simmer over low heat for about 15 minutes.

3 Cut the remaining root vegetables into matchsticks. Cook them in a little salted water for about 3 minutes, until tender but still crisp.

4 Transfer the cooked fish to warmed serving plates and arrange the vegetable matchsticks on top. Serve sprinkled with grated horseradish and, if you like, sprigs of parsley.

Note: Carp, a freshwater fish, is very popular in central Europpean cooking. There are several different varieties of carp: some are completely covered with scales; others, such as the mirror carp, have only a few large scales, while the leather carp has hardly any scales at all.

Wine: Dry white wine, such as one from the Burgenland region, goes well with carp.

Bregenzer Felchenfilets

Simple • Summer dish **Trout fillets with mushroom sauce** *Serves 4*

8 trout fillets (about 100 g each)
2 tbsp lemon juice
freshly ground white pepper
200 g mushrooms
1 small onion
15 g flat-leaf parsley
1 tbsp capers
60 g butter
4 tbsp dry white wine
salt
12.5 cl whipping cream

Preparation time: 45 minutes

1,800 kJ/430 calories per portion

1 Wash the trout fillets, pat dry and sprinkle with the lemon juice and a little pepper. Cover the fish and leave to stand in the refrigerator for about 10 minutes.

2 Meanwhile, clean and very thinly slice the mushrooms. Peel and finely chop the onion. Wash the parsley, shake dry and chop finely. Finely chop the capers.

3 Heat 30 g butter in a frying pan and fry the onion until transparent. Add the mushrooms and stir-fry over high heat for about 5 minutes, until almost all the liquid has evaporated.

4 Add the capers, parsley and wine to the mushroom mixture. Bring to the boil, then remove from the heat.

5 Heat the remaining butter in another frying pan. Season the trout fillets with salt, then fry them for 2 to 4 minutes on each side.

6 Stir the cream into the mushroom mixture, season with salt and pepper and heat to just below boiling point.

7 Arrange the fish on four serving plates and pour the sauce over the fish. Serve with boiled potatoes.

Hechtnockerln in Dillrahm

Quenelles with dill sauce

70 g white bread, crusts removed
25 cl whipping cream
1 medium-sized onion
30 g butter
350 g pike fillet
1 egg
salt
freshly ground white pepper
freshly grated nutmeg
¾ litre fish stock, or lightly salted water
30 g fresh dill
1 tbsp flour
4 tbsp soured cream
1 tbsp lemon juice

Preparation time: 1 ¼ hours

1,200 kJ/290 calories per portion (if serving 6)

1 Cut the bread into small dice and put in a bowl. Pour the cream over it and leave to soak in the refrigerator while preparing the fish.

2 Peel and finely chop the onion. Heat 15 g butter in a frying pan and fry half the chopped onion until transparent. Leave to cool. Reserve the rest of the onion for making the sauce.

3 Remove any bones from the pike fillet (*above*). Rinse the fish under cold running water, pat dry and cut into thin strips.

4 Using a fine blade, mince the fish strips and the fried onion twice. Alternatively, chop it finely in a food processor or blender. Transfer the fish mixture to a bowl and stir in the bread and cream.

5 Add the egg and season with salt, pepper and a little nutmeg. Press the mixture through a sieve, then leave to stand and firm up for a few minutes in the refrigerator.

6 Bring the fish stock or salted water to the boil in a wide saucepan.

7 Using a tablespoon dipped first in hot water, shape the mixture into long quenelles (*above*), and gently lower them into the stock or water. Simmer, uncovered, over low heat for about 10 minutes.

8 Meanwhile, wash the dill and shake dry; set aside a few sprigs for the garnish. Reserve the stems and finely chop the leaves.

9 Remove the quenelles from the saucepan, drain thoroughly and keep warm. Reserve about half the stock for making the sauce (the remainder can be kept for making soups or sauces).

10 Heat the remaining butter in a frying pan and fry the reserved onion until transparent. Sprinkle the flour over the top, then pour in the fish stock. Add the dill stems, bring to the boil, then remove from the heat.

11 Strain the sauce through a sieve and stir in the soured cream. Add the dill leaves and season with salt, pepper and the lemon juice. Pour the sauce onto individual plates and arrange the quenelles on top. Garnish with sprigs of dill.

Wiener Backhendl

Easy • Supper dish   **Chicken fried in breadcrumbs**   *Serves 4*

4 large chicken joints
salt
2 eggs
100 g flour
150 g fresh breadcrumbs
250 to 300 g pork dripping, or
25 cl vegetable oil
30 g flat-leaf parsley
1 unwaxed lemon

Preparation time: 1 hour

4,100kJ/980 calories per portion

1 Rinse the chicken joints, pat dry and season lightly with salt. Whisk the eggs in a soup plate. Pour the flour and breadcrumbs onto separate plates.

2 Coat the chicken joints in flour. Dip them in the beaten egg, draining off the excess, then coat in breadcrumbs.

3 Heat the dripping or oil in a deep-fat fryer or large frying pan. Fry the chicken joints, one at a time, for 12 to 15 minutes, until golden. Turn them half way through the cooking time.

4 Remove the cooked chicken from the pan, drain on paper towels and keep warm.

5 Wash the parsley, shake dry, then fry in the fat for 1 minute. Wash the lemon in hot water, then cut it into eight wedges.

6 Arrange the chicken joints on warmed individual plates. Serve garnished with the parsley and the lemon wedges.

Note: Chicken joints are very convenient, but they are a more expensive way of buying chicken. If preferred, buy two 800 g chickens and divide each of them into four joints.

Wine: Choose a spicy, flowery white wine, such as a Grüner Veltliner from the Wachau, to accompany this dish.

 # Gefüllte Gans

Takes time • Dinner party dish

Roast goose with chestnut and apple stuffing

Serves 8

250 g raw chestnuts
salt
500 g small tart apples
1 oven-ready goose (about 4 kg)
freshly ground black pepper
1 tbsp dried marjoram
sautéed apple wedges for garnish
(optional)

Preparation time: 1 hour
(plus 3½ hours' cooking time)

7,500 kJ/1,800 calories per portion

1 Wash the chestnuts. Using a sharp knife, make a small lengthwise incision on the plumper side of each nut. Cook in lightly salted water over medium heat for about 25 minutes, until tender.

2 Peel, quarter and core the apples. Rinse the goose under cold running water, then pat dry. Rub inside and out with salt and pepper; rub the inside with the dried marjoram.

3 Preheat the oven to 200°C (400°F or Mark 6). Drain the chestnuts, remove the shells and brown inner skin. Stuff the goose with the chestnuts and apples. Sew up the body cavity with kitchen twine. Bring about ¼ litre water to the boil.

4 Place the goose, breast downwards, in a large roasting pan, and pour over the boiling water. Roast on the bottom shelf of the oven for about 1¾ hours, basting every 15 minutes or so. Turn the goose on its back and continue roasting for a further 1¾ hours, until crisp and brown and the juices run clear when a fine skewer is inserted into the thickest part of the thigh.

5 Carve the cooked goose into eight portions. Add a little water to the juices in the roasting pan. Bring to the boil and skim off the fat. Serve the goose accompanied by the stuffing, with the gravy served separately. Garnish, if you like, with sautéed apple wedges.

Drink: Serve with a robust red wine.

HOME COOKING

Throughout the Austrian countryside there is a tradition of simple, wholesome cooking, many of whose dishes have found their way onto the menus of city-dwellers.

Today, the robust fare typical of these rural areas is popular not only with restaurateurs, but with all those who enjoy hearty, uncomplicated food. At the same time, these traditional dishes are ideal for the health-conscious, or vegetarians, since many of them contain little or no meat. Some of the dishes in this chapter are a blend of both rural and urban cooking styles, others a combination of Bohemian, Italian and Hungarian cuisines.

For a quick meal, try the savoury filled pasta specialities such as *Kärtner Kasnudeln, Schlutzkrapfen* and *Sauerkrattirteln.* For a delicious, meatless feast, try *Käsespätzle,* served with a fresh green salad. There are dishes here to suit every appetite, with no need for any side dish, making them an easy, economical way of catering for a large number of guests.

Schinkenfleckerln

Pasta squares baked with ham

Serves 4

300 g flour
5 eggs
salt
200 g lean cooked ham, in one piece
1 medium-sized onion
30 g softened butter, plus 15 g straight from the refrigerator
1 tbsp vegetable oil
2 tbsp fresh breadcrumbs
30 g flat-leaf parsley
12.5 cl soured cream
freshly grated nutmeg
freshly ground black pepper

Preparation time: 1¾ hours
(plus 30 minutes' standing time)

2,900 kJ/690 calories per portion

1 Sift the flour into a heap on a work surface. Make a well in the middle. Break 3 eggs into the well and add a little salt. Work the flour quickly into the middle to make a smooth dough. If necessary, add a little cold water so that the ingredients blend well together.

2 Continue to knead the dough with the balls of the thumbs for about 15 minutes, until it is smooth and shiny. Place an upturned bowl over the dough and leave to stand for about 30 minutes.

3 On a lightly floured surface, roll out the dough thinly and leave for about 10 minutes to dry out.

4 Meanwhile, chop the ham fairly finely. Peel and finely chop the onion. Heat the 30 g butter in a frying pan and fry the onion until transparent, then leave to cool.

5 Cut the pastry first lengthwise and then crosswise to make 1 cm squares (*fleckerln*).

6 Bring about 3 litres of water to the boil in a large saucepan. Add the oil and 1½ tsp salt. Cook the *fleckerln* for about 6 minutes, until tender but still firm to the bite. Strain through a large colander and drain thoroughly.

7 Preheat the oven to 200°C (400°F or Mark 6). Butter an ovenproof baking dish and sprinkle it with half the breadcrumbs.

8 Wash the parsley, shake dry, remove the stalks and finely chop the leaves.

9 Separate the remaining 2 eggs. Whisk the yolks in a bowl with the soured cream. Stir in the drained *fleckerln*, chopped ham and onion, including the butter in which they have been cooked. Add the chopped parsley and a little nutmeg, and season with salt and pepper. Whisk the egg whites until stiff, then carefully fold them into the mixture.

10 Transfer the mixture to the baking dish and sprinkle with the remaining breadcrumbs. Cut the 15 g cold butter into slivers and dot them over the top.

11 Bake in the centre of the oven for about 30 minutes, until golden-brown. Serve with a green salad.

Variation: Krautfleckerln

(Pasta squares with cabbage)
Cut a small white cabbage into quarters and wash under cold running water. Remove the main stalk, then finely grate the cabbage leaves. Heat 45 g butter in a frying pan and fry 1 medium-sized, finely chopped onion until transparent. Sprinkle 1 tbsp sugar over the onion and cook until caramelized. Add 1 tbsp wine vinegar and pour over 12.5 cl hot meat stock or water. Add the cabbage and cook for about 30 minutes, stirring frequently. Season with salt, pepper and 1 tsp ground caraway seeds. Stir the cooked *fleckerln* into the cabbage, and serve immediately.

Kärtner Kasnudeln

Cheap but takes time • Carinthia

Quark-filled pasta pockets

Serves 4

300 g flour
3 eggs
salt
120 g floury potatoes, scrubbed but not peeled
250 g quark
2 tbsp soured cream
2 tbsp chopped fresh herbs (parsley, chervil, a little mint)
freshly grated nutmeg
freshly ground black pepper
1 egg white
100 g rindless smoked bacon

Preparation time: 1¼ hours

2,500 kJ/600 calories per portion

1 Sift the flour into a heap on a work surface. Make a well in the middle. Break the eggs into the well and add a little salt. Work the flour quickly into the middle to make a smooth dough, adding a little water, if necessary. Knead for 15 minutes, then cover and leave to stand for about 30 minutes.

2 Meanwhile, boil the potatoes until soft, then peel and mash finely while still hot. Add the quark and soured cream. Season with the herbs, a little nutmeg, salt and pepper.

3 On a lightly floured surface, roll out the pastry until about 2 mm thick. Using an 8 cm plain pastry cutter or a glass, cut the pastry into circles. Place

1 tsp of filling in the centre of each circle. Brush the edges with egg white.

4 Fold the circles in half, pressing the edges firmly together. Mark all round the edges with the back of a knife or the handle of a fork.

5 Bring plenty of salted water to the boil in a large saucepan. Add the *kasnudeln* to the boiling water and simmer over medium heat for about 10 minutes. Meanwhile, cut the bacon into small dice or strips and fry over medium heat until crisp.

6 Remove the *kasnudeln* from the water and serve sprinkled with the pieces of crispy bacon.

Schlutzkrapfen

More complex • Tyrol

Pasta pockets with spinach filling

Serves 4

300 g flour
4 eggs
salt
300 g leaf spinach
125 g quark
100 g Emmenthal cheese, grated
freshly grated nutmeg
freshly ground white pepper
1 egg white
30 g butter
½ bunch chives

Preparation time: 1¼ hours

2,500 kJ/600 calories per portion

1 Sift the flour into a heap on a work surface. Make a well in the middle. Break 3 eggs into the well and add a little salt. Work the flour quickly into the middle to make a smooth dough, adding a little water, if necessary. Knead for 15 minutes, then cover and leave to stand for about 30 minutes.

2 Meanwhile, wash the spinach and blanch briefly in a small quantity of boiling water. Drain, squeeze out the water, then chop. Mix with the quark, 50 g cheese and the remaining egg. Season with nutmeg, salt and pepper.

3 On a lightly floured surface, roll out the pastry until about 2 mm thick.

Using an 8 cm plain pastry cutter or a glass, cut the pastry into circles. Place 1 tsp of filling in the centre of each circle. Brush the edges with egg white. Fold the circles in half, pressing the edges firmly together.

4 Bring plenty of salted water to the boil in a large saucepan. Add the *schlutzkrapfen* and simmer over medium heat for about 10 minutes. Melt the butter. Wash the chives, shake dry and cut into tiny pieces. Remove the *schlutzkrapfen* from the water and arrange on a serving dish. Drizzle the melted butter over the top and sprinkle with the remaining grated cheese and the finely cut chives.

Sauerkrauttirteln

Little sauerkraut pies

300 g flour
3 eggs
salt
250 g sauerkraut
1 small onion
30 g butter
15 g flat-leaf parsley
1 egg white
150 g clarified butter (see Glossary),
or 15 cl vegetable oil

Preparation time: 1 hour

2,400 kJ/570 calories per portion

1 Sift the flour into a heap on a work surface. Make a well in the middle. Break the eggs into the well and add a little salt. Work the flour quickly into the middle to make a smooth dough, adding a little water, if necessary. Knead the dough with the balls of the thumbs for about 15 minutes, then cover and leave to stand for about 30 minutes.

2 Finely chop the sauerkraut. Peel and finely chop the onion. Heat the butter and fry the chopped onion until transparent. Add the sauerkraut and stir-fry over medium heat for about 5 minutes. Remove from the heat and leave to cool. Wash the parsley, shake dry, remove the stalks and finely chop the leaves. Stir the leaves into the cooled sauerkraut and season with salt.

3 Whisk the egg white. On a lightly floured surface, roll out the pastry until about 2 mm thick. Using a 10 cm plain pastry cutter or a glass, cut the pastry into circles. Take half of the circles and place 1 tsp of filling in the centre of each one. Brush the edges with egg white. Place a second circle on top of each of the filled ones, pressing the edges firmly together.

4 Heat the clarified butter or oil in a large frying pan. Fry the pies over medium heat for about 3 minutes on each side, until golden-brown. Remove the pies from the pan, drain on paper towels, and serve.

Drink: Serve with cold beer.

Eiernockerln
Egg dumplings

Serves 4

salt
300 g flour
7 eggs
about 20 cl milk
freshly grated nutmeg
1 bunch chives
30 g butter

Preparation time: 30 minutes

2,600 kJ/620 calories per portion

1 Bring plenty of salted water to the boil in a large saucepan.

2 Place the flour, 3 eggs, the milk and a little nutmeg and salt in a bowl and mix to a smooth, not-too-firm dough. Add a little more milk, if necessary. Using a tablespoon dipped first in hot water, shape the dough into oval dumplings about 4 cm long. Lower the dumplings into the boiling water and simmer over low heat for about 8 minutes.

3 Meanwhile, whisk the remaining eggs in a bowl. Wash the chives, shake dry and cut into tiny pieces. Heat the butter in a large frying pan.

4 Drain the dumplings in a large colander. Add them to the hot butter and toss until coated. Pour the beaten egg over the dumplings in the pan and season lightly with salt. Cook briefly until the egg starts to set.

5 Sprinkle with the finely cut chives and serve immediately, accompanied by a green salad.

Drink: Serve with cold beer.

Käsespätzle

Easy • Vorarlberg

Batter strips with onion rings and cheese

Serves 4

salt
2 medium-sized onions
400 g flour
4 eggs
about 20 cl milk
freshly grated nutmeg
60 g butter
200 g tasty cheese (for example, Emmenthal)

Preparation time: 40 minutes

3,500 kJ/830 calories per portion

1 Preheat the oven to its lowest setting. Bring plenty of salted water to the boil in a large saucepan. Peel the onions and cut them into thin rings.

2 Place the flour, 3 eggs, the milk and a little nutmeg and salt in a bowl and mix to a smooth, not-too-firm dough. Add a little more milk, if necessary. Pat out the dough on a dampened chopping board, then cut it into short, thin strips with a knife. Place the strips immediately in the boiling water and simmer for a few minutes. When cooked, they will float to the surface.

3 Meanwhile, melt 30 g butter in a large frying pan. Warm a baking dish in the oven. Grate the cheese.

4 Remove the *spätzle* from the water with a slotted spoon, drain, then add to the melted butter and toss until coated. Arrange the *spätzle* in the warmed baking dish, layering them alternately with the grated cheese. Cover the dish and leave in the centre of the oven for about 5 minutes to melt the cheese.

5 Heat the remaining butter in a frying pan and fry the onions over medium heat until golden-brown. Sprinkle the onion rings over the *spätzle* and serve at once.

Wine: Serve with a full-bodied red or white wine.

Tiroler Gröstl

Not difficult • Supper dish

Fried potatoes with pork or ham

Serves 4

600 g cold, boiled potatoes
1 medium-sized onion
300 g roast pork, or cooked ham
80 g pork dripping, or butter
salt
freshly ground black pepper
1 tsp dried marjoram
30 g flat-leaf parsley
30 g butter
4 eggs

Preparation time: 40 minutes
(plus boiling and cooling time for the potatoes)

2,100 kJ/500 calories per portion

1 Peel and thinly slice the potatoes. Peel and finely chop the onion. Cut the pork or ham into small dice.

2 Heat the dripping or butter in a large frying pan and fry the onion until lightly browned. Add the potato slices and the pork or ham. Season with salt, pepper and the marjoram, then sauté over medium heat for about 15 minutes, stirring frequently, until the potatoes begin to brown.

3 Wash the parsley, shake dry, remove the stalks and finely chop the leaves. Sprinkle the chopped leaves over the potatoes.

4 Heat the butter in another pan and fry the eggs. Sprinkle with salt and serve immediately, accompanied by the fried potatoes and a green salad.

Variation:
Stockfischgröstl
(Fried potatoes with salt cod)
Instead of meat, use 500 g salt cod. Soak the salt cod overnight in cold water. The following day, simmer the fish in fresh salted water over low heat for about 20 minutes, until tender. Remove the skin and bones and break the flesh into bite-sized pieces. Fry 1 finely chopped garlic clove with the onion. Omit the marjoram and eggs. Stir in 4 tbsp cream before serving.

Erdäpfelgulasch mit Speck

Easy • Lightly spicy · **Potato and bacon goulash** · *Serves 4*

750 g floury potatoes
2 medium-sized onions
100 g rindless, smoked streaky bacon
30 g pork dripping, or 2 tbsp vegetable oil
2 tbsp mild paprika
1 tbsp wine vinegar
about 1 litre beef stock (see page 23), or water
2 bay leaves
½ tsp ground caraway seeds
1 tsp dried marjoram
1 garlic clove • salt
freshly ground black pepper

Preparation time: 1 hour

1,400 kJ/330 calories per portion

1 Peel and wash the potatoes and cut them into large dice. Peel and finely chop the onions. Cut the bacon into small dice.

2 Heat the dripping or oil in a large frying pan and fry the chopped onions and diced bacon until the onions are transparent. Sprinkle the paprika over the top and immediately add the vinegar and about 3 tbsp beef stock or water. Add the bay leaves, caraway and marjoram. Peel and crush the garlic and add it to the pan. Stir in the diced potatoes and add just enough stock or water to cover the potatoes. Cover the frying pan and then cook over medium heat for about 30 minutes.

3 Discard the bay leaves and season with salt and pepper.

Drink: Serve the goulash with a cold beer or lager, either alcoholic or non-alcoholic.

Note: If the cooked potato goulash has too much liquid, remove a few potatoes, purée them, then stir the purée into the pan. To make the sauce creamier, stir in 2 tbsp crème fraîche or soured cream.

For added flavour, slice 200 g smoked sausage and add it to the pan shortly before the end of the cooking time.

Eierschwammerlgulasch

Quick and easy • Vegetarian dish · **Chanterelles in cream sauce** · *Serves 4*

500 g chanterelle mushrooms
1 large onion
2 garlic cloves
30 g flat-leaf parsley
30 g butter
1 tbsp lemon juice
½ litre vegetable stock (or use stock cubes)
1 tbsp mild paprika
4 tbsp soured cream
salt
freshly ground black pepper

Preparation time: 45 minutes

510 kJ/120 calories per portion

1 Clean and trim the chanterelles, cutting the larger ones in half. Peel and finely chop the onion and garlic. Wash the parsley, shake dry, remove the stalks and finely chop the leaves.

2 Heat the butter in a large saucepan and fry the onion and garlic until the onion is transparent. Add the parsley and chanterelles and cook over medium heat for about 10 minutes, stirring from time to time.

3 Stir in the lemon juice, vegetable stock and paprika. Bring to the boil and cook over low heat for about 10 minutes, until the chanterelles are cooked. Stir in the soured cream and season with salt and pepper.

Variation: Eierschwammerlpfanne (Chanterelle pancake)
Chop 100 g smoked streaky bacon into small dice and fry until the fat runs. Fry 1 chopped small onion and 400 g thinly sliced boiled potatoes in the bacon fat over medium heat for about 15 minutes. Trim and clean 300 g chanterelles, add to the potatoes and cook for about 10 minutes. Season with salt and pepper. Whisk 4 eggs with 2 tbsp milk, pour over the potatoes and cook until the egg is set. Sprinkle with chopped parsley.

Krautwickel

More complex • Economical

Stuffed cabbage rolls

1 day-old bread roll
12.5 cl litre milk
salt
1 white or savoy cabbage
(about 800 g)
1 small onion
2 garlic cloves
30 g butter
30 g flat-leaf parsley
400 g minced beef and pork, mixed
dried marjoram
1 egg
freshly ground black pepper
12.5 cl beef stock (see page 23; or
use stock cubes)
2 tbsp soured cream

Preparation time: 1¼ hours

1,900 kJ/450 calories per portion

1 Grate off the crust of the bread roll. Dice the roll and soak it in the milk. Bring plenty of salted water to the boil in a saucepan.

2 Discard the damaged outer leaves of the white or savoy cabbage and cut out the main stalk with a sharp knife. Wash the cabbage and place it in the boiling water. Swirl the water with a fork to loosen the cabbage leaves, then simmer over low heat for about 15 minutes, until it begins to soften.

3 Meanwhile, peel and chop the onion and garlic. Heat the butter in a frying pan and fry the onion and garlic until the onion is transparent. Leave to cool.

4 Wash the parsley, shake dry, remove the stalks and chop the leaves. Squeeze the moisture from the soaked bread. Put the bread in a bowl and mix in the minced beef and pork, the onion, garlic, chopped parsley and a little marjoram. Add the egg and mix thoroughly. Season with salt and pepper.

5 Preheat the oven to 200°C (400°F or Mark 6). Butter an ovenproof dish. Bring the beef stock to the boil.

6 Remove the cabbage leaves from the water and drain thoroughly on paper towels. Any thick, protruding ribs should be pared flat, so that the leaves can easily be rolled up.

7 Place 1 tbsp of the stuffing in the centre of each leaf. Fold the edges inwards, then roll the leaves into small parcels (*below*). Secure each one with a toothpick, if necessary. Pack the

cabbage rolls closely together in the baking dish with the join downwards. Cover with the hot beef stock.

8 Cover the dish and cook in the bottom of the oven for 30 minutes. Remove the cabbage rolls from the dish and keep warm.

9 Strain the cooking juices through a sieve into a small saucepan. Stir in the soured cream and heat to just below boiling point, but do not allow to boil.

10 Serve the stuffed cabbage rolls with the sauce, accompanied by boiled potatoes, sprinkled, if you like, with a little chopped parsley.

Drink: Beer is an excellent choice to accompany this dish.

Krautstrudel

White cabbage strudel

Serves 4

200 g flour
1 egg
1 tbsp vegetable oil
salt
1 small onion
1 white cabbage (about 800 g)
30 g pork dripping, or butter
1 tbsp sugar
1 tbsp white wine vinegar
about 12.5 cl beef stock (see page 23; or use stock cubes), or water
1 tsp ground caraway seeds
freshly ground black pepper
12.5 cl soured cream
about 50 g butter

Preparation time: 2 hours

1,900 kJ/450 calories per portion

1 Sift the flour into a heap on a work surface. Make a well in the middle. Break the egg into the well and add the oil and a little salt. Work the flour into the middle to make a smooth dough, adding up to 3 tbsp warm water, a little at a time, until the dough is fairly firm.

2 Knead the dough with the balls of the thumbs for about 15 minutes, until smooth and shiny. Shape the dough into a ball, brush with oil, cover with an upturned bowl, and leave to stand for about 30 minutes.

3 Meanwhile, make the filling. Peel and finely chop the onion. Remove the damaged outer leaves of the cabbage and cut it into quarters, discarding the central stalk. Wash the cabbage and finely grate or shred the leaves.

4 Heat the dripping or butter in a large frying pan and fry the chopped onion until transparent. Sprinkle with sugar and cook until caramelized. Add the vinegar and beef stock, or water. Add the cabbage and caraway and season to taste with salt and pepper.

5 Cover the pan and cook over low heat for about 20 minutes, until the cabbage begins to soften, stirring frequently to avoid burning. Add a little more stock or water, if necessary, but all the liquid should have evaporated by the end of the cooking time. Allow the cabbage to cool a little before stirring in the soured cream.

6 Spread a large cloth on a table and sprinkle evenly with flour. Roll out the dough as thinly as possible. Flour the backs of both your hands. Carefully place the backs of the hands under the dough and stretch outwards from the middle until the dough is paper thin and transparent enough to be able to read a newspaper through it. Cut off the thick edges of the dough.

7 Melt the butter in a frying pan. Brush a baking sheet with some of the melted butter and reserve the rest. Preheat the oven to 200°C (400°F or Mark 6).

8 Thinly brush the strudel dough with melted butter. Spread the cabbage filling evenly over the dough, leaving a margin of about 3 cm all round. Lift the cloth and roll up the strudel, folding the sides inwards. Place the strudel on the greased baking sheet, with the join downwards; make it into a horseshoe shape, if you like.

9 Brush the strudel with melted butter and bake in the centre of the oven for about 45 minutes, until golden-brown. Cut into pieces about 8 cm wide and serve immediately.

Note: Strudel pastry is fairly difficult and time consuming to make. If preferred, use frozen filo pastry, which is widely available in supermarkets.

Gefüllte Paprika

Simple • Family dish **Stuffed peppers** *Serves 4*

4 large green, red or yellow sweet peppers
1 medium-sized onion
2 tbsp vegetable oil
400 g minced beef and pork, mixed
100 g cooked rice
1 egg
1 tsp dried marjoram
1 garlic clove
30 g flat-leaf parsley
salt
about ¼ litre beef stock (see page 23; or use stock cubes)
12.5 cl soured cream
4 tbsp tomato purée
hot paprika

Preparation time: 1 hour

1,900 kJ/450 calories per portion

1 Wash the peppers and slice off the tops to make "lids". Remove the seeds and ribs. Peel and finely chop the onion. Heat the oil in a frying pan and fry the onion until transparent. Add the meat and stir-fry over high heat until it has lost its colour, then remove from the heat.

2 Add the cooked rice, egg and marjoram to the meat. Peel and crush the garlic and add it to the meat mixture. Wash the parsley, shake dry, remove the stalks and finely chop the leaves. Add the chopped leaves to the meat, season with a little salt and mix well. Fill the peppers with the meat mixture and then place the "lids" on top. Bring the beef stock to the boil in a small saucepan.

3 Place the stuffed peppers in a wide saucepan, then pour the beef stock around them. Cover the pan and cook over low heat for about 40 minutes. If necessary, add a little more stock. Remove the cooked peppers from the pan, arrange them on a warmed serving dish and keep warm.

4 Stir the soured cream and tomato purée into the pepper's cooking liquid and heat through. Season with a little paprika and salt. Serve the stuffed peppers accompanied, if you like, by boiled potatoes, with the tomato sauce served separately.

Drink: Serve with apple or grape juice, or a light red wine, such as one from the Burgenland region.

Peppers

The pepper family ranges from tiny hot chili peppers to large, mild sweet varieties, of which the most familiar are the sweet green variety at right and the riper, red version. Today, even more colourful varieties have been developed, so that now yellow, orange, black and purple peppers can commonly be found.

A versatile vegetable, rich in vitamin C, peppers can be used raw in salads, cooked as a vegetable, or marinated in olive oil. The larger ones are very good for stuffing.

To skin raw peppers, place them under a hot grill until the skins are scorched and blistered. Then put them in a covered bowl or closed paper bag. When cool enough to handle, carefully peel off the skin with a paring knife.

Look for peppers with firm, smooth and shiny skins; they will keep in the vegetable compartment of the refrigerator for up to 3 days.

250 g

Topfen

besonders fein

Tauernmilch
Bischofshofen

430 kJ/100g
103 kcal/100g
extra streichfähig
rahmmilch, delikat

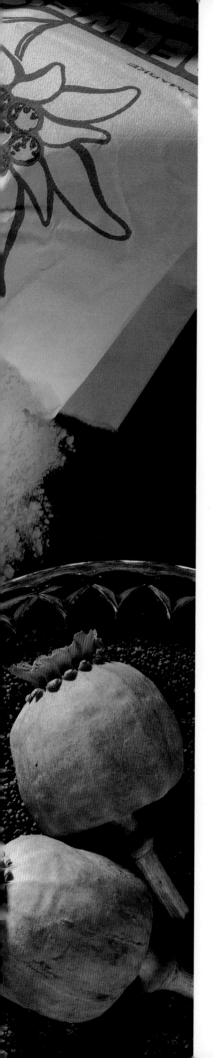

SWEET DUMPLINGS AND PASTRIES

The first image that springs to anyone's mind when they think of Austrian cookery is its glorious, unrivalled pâtisserie: the cakes, pastries and puddings all enticingly displayed in the countless little pastry shops and coffee houses for which the country is famed.

The essential ingredient in all of these delicacies is sugar, which was first brought to Austria from India during the 16th century. For several hundred years, however, such sweet delicacies were largely the preserve of the nobility; it was not until the 19th century that sugar became cheap enough for the rest of the population to begin using it on a regular basis, and cakes and pastries took their place on the everyday menu.

The secret of successful dumplings and pastries is simple, good-quality ingredients, such as fine flour, and care in the preparation. In Austria it is customary to serve such dishes as *Strudel, Knödel, Tascherln, Buchteln* and *Nockerln* as the centrepiece of a meal. Of course, they also make excellent—and filling—desserts.

Apfelstrudel
Apple and raisin strudel

Serves 12

200 g flour
1 egg
1 tbsp vegetable oil
salt
60 g raisins
2 tbsp rum
140 g butter
80 g fresh breadcrumbs
1.5 kg tart eating apples
about 100 g caster sugar
1 tsp ground cinnamon
icing sugar for sprinkling

Preparation time: 2¼ hours

1,200 kJ/290 calories per portion

1 Sift the flour into a heap on a work surface. Make a well in the middle. Break the egg into the well and add the oil and salt. Work the flour into the middle to make a smooth dough, gradually adding up to 3 tbsp lukewarm water to obtain a fairly firm consistency. Knead the dough with the balls of the thumbs, until it is smooth and shiny. Shape the dough into a ball and brush with a little oil. Cover with an upturned bowl, then leave to stand for about 30 minutes.

2 Meanwhile, wash the raisins, pat them dry and put in a bowl. Sprinkle with the rum, cover and set aside. Heat 40 g butter in a frying pan and stir-fry the breadcrumbs until they are golden-brown. Leave to cool. Peel, core and thinly slice the apples. Mix the caster sugar and cinnamon together in a bowl. If the apples are very tart, add a little extra sugar.

3 Spread a large cloth on a table and sprinkle evenly with flour. Roll out the dough as thinly as possible. Flour the backs of both your hands. Carefully place the backs of the hands under the dough and stretch outwards from the middle until the dough is paper thin and transparent enough to be able to read a newspaper through it. Cut off the thick edges of the dough.

4 Melt the remaining butter in a frying pan. Use some of the butter to brush a baking sheet. Preheat the oven to 200°C (400°F or Mark 6).

5 Sprinkle the fried breadcrumbs over about two thirds of the rolled out pastry, leaving a strip about 3 cm wide along each of the two edges that will become the ends of the strudel. Brush the uncovered third with melted butter. Arrange the sliced apples over the breadcrumbs and sprinkle with the cinnamon sugar and raisins. Fold the uncovered strip over the filling, so it does not leak. Lift the cloth and roll up

the strudel, so that the part covered by the unfilled strip is rolled in last. Slide the strudel, with the join downwards, onto the greased baking sheet. Make it into a horseshoe shape, if you like.

6 Brush the strudel with melted butter and bake in the centre of the oven for 35 to 45 minutes, until golden-brown, brushing with melted butter about every 10 minutes.

7 Cut into slices, 4 to 5 cm wide. Sprinkle with icing sugar and serve, preferably while it is still warm.

Note: Strudel pastry is fairly difficult and time consuming to make. If preferred, use frozen filo pastry, which is widely available in supermarkets.

Variation:
Wachauer Marillenstrudel
(Apricot strudel)
Instead of apples, use 1.5 kg stoned, halved apricots, and omit the raisins and rum. Bake for about 45 minutes.

Topfenstrudel

Quark strudel

200 g flour

4 eggs

1 tbsp vegetable oil

salt

about 3 tbsp lukewarm water

50 g raisins

1 tbsp rum

500 g quark

100 g caster sugar, plus 1 tbsp for glazing

2 tsp vanilla sugar (see Note)

grated rind of ½ unwaxed lemon

about 80 g butter

2 tbsp fresh breadcrumbs

12.5 cl milk

1 egg yolk

4 tbsp icing sugar

Preparation time: 2 hours

1,400 kJ/330 calories per portion

1 Sift the flour into a heap on a work surface. Make a well in the middle. Break 1 egg into the well and add the oil and salt. Work the flour into the middle to make a smooth dough, gradually adding up to 3 tbsp warm water to obtain a firmish consistency.

2 Knead the dough with the balls of the thumbs for about 15 minutes, until it is smooth and shiny. Divide the dough in half, shape into two balls and brush with oil. Cover with an upturned bowl and leave to stand for about 30 minutes.

3 Meanwhile, wash the raisins, pat dry and put in a bowl. Sprinkle with the rum, cover and reserve.

4 When the dough has been standing for nearly 30 minutes, mix the quark in a bowl with the caster sugar and half the vanilla sugar. Separate the 3 eggs, stir the yolks into the quark, then add the lemon rind and raisins. Whisk the egg whites with a little salt until stiff, then fold into the quark mixture.

5 Melt the butter in a saucepan. Use some of the melted butter to grease a large, rectangular baking dish and reserve the rest.

6 Spread a large cloth on a table and sprinkle evenly with flour. Take one ball of dough, and roll out as thinly as possible. Flour the backs of both your hands. Carefully place the backs of your hands under the dough and stretch outwards from the middle, until the dough is paper thin and transparent enough to be able to read a newspaper

through it. Cut off the thick edges of the dough.

7 Thinly brush the strudel pastry with the melted butter, then sprinkle with 1 tbsp breadcrumbs. Spread half the filling over the pastry, leaving a 3 cm border all round. Fold the ends inwards, then raise the cloth and roll up the strudel. Slide the strudel into the baking dish, with the join downwards.

8 Preheat the oven to 200°C (400°F or Mark 6). Repeat the process with the second ball of dough, and place it alongside the first strudel in the baking dish. Brush both strudels with melted butter. Place the dish in the centre of the oven and bake for about 30 minutes.

9 To make the glaze, whisk the remaining egg yolk with 1 tbsp caster sugar and the remaining vanilla sugar. Brush the glaze over the strudels and bake for a further 15 minutes, until golden.

10 Cut the two strudels into slices, 4 to 5 cm wide, and sprinkle with the icing sugar. Serve while still warm, accompanied by vanilla custard (*recipe, page 100*).

Note: To make vanilla sugar, fill a jar with sugar and add a vanilla pod. Leave the sugar for two to three weeks, to absorb the vanilla flavour. Keep the jar topped up with sugar so that you always have some ready for use.

Strudel pastry is difficult and time consuming to make; if you prefer, frozen filo pastry can be used instead.

Germknödel mit Mohn

Yeast dumplings with poppy seeds

Takes time • Economical

Serves 4

For the dumplings:
250 g flour
20 g fresh, or 2 tsp dried, yeast
1 tbsp caster sugar
6 tbsp lukewarm milk
1 egg
grated rind of ½ unwaxed lemon
salt

For the filling and coating:
4 tbsp plum purée (see Note)
60 g butter
50 g poppy seeds
2 tbsp icing sugar

Preparation time: 45 minutes
(plus 1 hour for proving)

2,200 kJ/520 calories per portion

1 All the dumpling ingredients must be at warm room temperature.

2 Sift the flour into a large bowl and make a well in the middle. Crumble the fresh yeast into the well. Add the caster sugar and a little lukewarm milk to the yeast and stir well, then sprinkle with a little flour from around the edge. Cover and leave in a warm place until cracks can be seen in the flour. This takes about 15 minutes. If using dried yeast, sprinkle it into a little of the milk with the sugar, leave until frothy, then add to the flour.

3 Whisk the egg with the rest of the milk. Add the lemon rind and a little salt. Add the mixture to the dough in the bowl and beat in the flour to make a smooth yeast dough. If necessary, add a little more warm milk. The dough should be bubbly and come away easily from the sides of the bowl. Cover and leave to rise for 20 minutes.

4 Divide the dough into four equal-sized pieces and press them down flat. Place 1 tbsp plum purée in the middle of each piece. Shape into four large dumplings and leave to prove for a further 20 minutes.

5 Bring plenty of salted water to the boil in a large saucepan. If necessary, use two saucepans, as the dumplings swell considerably while cooking and they should not come into contact with each other.

6 Place the dumplings in the gently boiling water and simmer, uncovered, over low heat for about 12 minutes, turning them over half way through the cooking time. They are done when a fine skewer inserted into the centre comes out clean.

7 Melt the butter in a frying pan. Mix the poppy seeds with the icing sugar.

8 Remove the cooked dumplings from the water with a slotted spoon. Drain thoroughly, then prick several times with a fine skewer so that they do not sink too quickly. Place on warmed individual plates, pour over the melted butter, sprinkle with the sugared poppy seeds and serve immediately.

Note: It is worth making a large quantity of plum purée as it will keep in a cool, dark place for up to six months. Wash and stone 3 kg plums and place them in a large saucepan. Sprinkle with 500 g sugar and pour over 12.5 cl white wine vinegar. Leave to stand overnight. The following day, simmer over low heat for about 6 hours but do not stir the purée while it is cooking, otherwise it will burn. Pour into sterilized jars and cover each with a wax disc and a dampened round of cellophane.

Dukatenbuchteln

Yeast dumplings with vanilla custard

For the dumplings:
400 g flour
30 g fresh, or 1 tbsp dried, yeast
50 g caster sugar
about 20 cl lukewarm milk
130 g butter
3 egg yolks
grated rind of ½ unwaxed lemon
salt
2 tbsp icing sugar

For the vanilla custard:
2 egg yolks
4 tbsp caster sugar
1 vanilla pod
½ litre milk
1 tbsp cornflour

*Preparation time: 1 hour
(plus 1 hour for proving)*

3,800 kJ/900 calories per portion

1 All the dumpling ingredients must be at warm room temperature.

2 Sift the flour into a large bowl and make a well in the middle. Crumble the fresh yeast into the well. Add 1 tsp of the caster sugar and a little lukewarm milk to the yeast and stir well, then sprinkle with a little flour from around the edge. Cover and leave to rise in a warm place until cracks can be seen in the flour. This takes about 15 minutes. If using dried yeast, sprinkle it into a little of the milk with the sugar, leave until frothy, then add to the flour.

3 Melt 80 g butter in the rest of the warm milk. Dissolve the rest of the

caster sugar in the milk. Add the egg yolks, grated lemon rind and a little salt and mix thoroughly. Add the mixture to the yeast dough and stir in with the flour. Knead to a smooth dough, adding more warm milk, if necessary. The dough should be bubbly and come away easily from the edge of the bowl. Cover and leave to rise for about 20 minutes.

4 In a small frying pan, melt the remaining butter. Butter a 30 by 20 cm rectangular baking dish; reserve the rest of the butter.

5 Knead the dough again, then roll it out on a lightly floured surface until it

is about 12 mm thick. Using a plain 2.5 cm pastry cutter or a liqueur glass, cut the dough into circles. Arrange the circles in rows in the baking dish. Cover and leave to prove for a further 20 minutes.

6 Preheat the oven to 200°C (400°F or Mark 6). Brush the dumplings with the remaining melted butter. Place the baking dish on the lowest shelf of the oven and bake for about 30 minutes, until the dumplings are a pale golden colour.

7 Meanwhile, make the vanilla custard. Whisk the egg yolks and sugar in a bowl with a hand whisk, until frothy. Halve the vanilla pod lengthwise and scrape out the pulp with the point of a knife. Stir the pulp, cornflour and a little of the milk together, then stir in the rest of the milk. Pour into a saucepan, add the egg mixture and cook over low heat, stirring constantly, until the custard becomes creamy. Do not allow to boil, otherwise it will curdle.

8 Sprinkle the cooked dumplings with the icing sugar. Pour the hot vanilla custard onto four individual plates and arrange the dumplings on top.

Note: You can also make the dumplings a little larger and fill them with plum purée (*see Note, page 98*) or any kind of jam.

Powidltascherln

Not difficult • Economical

Plum turnovers in buttery breadcrumbs

Serves 4

600 g floury potatoes
125 g flour
30 g semolina
1 egg
salt
1 egg white
100 g plum purée (see Note, page 98)
50 g butter
3 tbsp fresh breadcrumbs
2 tbsp icing sugar

Preparation time: 1½ hours

1,800 kJ/430 calories per portion (if serving 4)

1 Boil the potatoes in their skins until soft, then peel and mash finely while they are still hot. Mix the potatoes, flour, semolina, egg and a little salt to a smooth dough and leave to stand for a few minutes.

2 Bring plenty of salted water to the boil in a large saucepan.

3 On a lightly floured surface, roll out the potato dough until it is about 3 mm thick. Using a glass about 9 cm in diameter, cut the dough into circles. Whisk the egg white with 1 tsp water and brush the edges of the pastry circles with the mixture. Place 1 tsp plum purée in the centre of each circle.

Fold into half-moon shapes, carefully pressing the edges firmly together.

4 Place the plum turnovers in the boiling water and simmer, uncovered, over low heat for 6 to 8 minutes.

5 Heat the butter in a frying pan and fry the breadcrumbs until golden-brown. Remove the turnovers from the water with a slotted spoon, drain on paper towels, then coat them in the buttery breadcrumbs. Serve sprinkled with the icing sugar.

Note: Served as a dessert, this quantity is enough for eight people.

Waldviertler Mohnnudeln

Easy • Economical

Potato dumplings with poppy-seed butter

Serves 4

600 g floury potatoes
100 g butter
200 g flour
50 g semolina
2 egg yolks
salt
120 g poppy seeds
4 tbsp icing sugar

Preparation time: 1¼ hours

2,900 kJ/690 calories per portion (if serving 4)

1 Boil the potatoes in their skins until soft, then peel and mash finely while still hot. Put the mashed potato in a large bowl. Add 50 g butter, the flour, semolina, egg yolks and a little salt and mix to a smooth dough. Leave to stand for a few minutes.

2 Bring plenty of salted water to the boil in a large saucepan.

3 On a floured surface, shape the dough into rolls about the thickness of your thumb, then cut into walnut-sized pieces. Form the pieces into sausage-shaped dumplings about 6 cm long and pointed at each end.

4 Place the dumplings in the gently boiling water and simmer, uncovered, over medium heat for about 6 minutes. Melt the remaining butter in a frying pan until it froths and briefly sauté the poppy seeds.

5 Remove the dumplings from the water with a slotted spoon, drain, then roll them in the buttered poppy seeds. Serve sprinkled with the icing sugar.

Variation: Instead of poppy seeds, use breadcrumbs or finely ground nuts.

Note: Served as a dessert, this quantity is enough for eight people.

Wachauer Marillenknödel

Apricot dumplings in buttery breadcrumbs

Takes time • Ideal for children

Serves 4

200 g quark
1 egg
50 g softened butter
150 g flour
grated rind of ½ unwaxed lemon
salt
8 small ripe apricots
8 cubes sugar
50 g butter
80 g fresh breadcrumbs
2 tbsp icing sugar

Preparation time: 45 minutes
(plus 30 minutes' standing time)

1,900 kJ/450 calories per portion

1 Put the quark, egg, butter, flour, lemon rind and a little salt in a bowl and mix to a smooth dough. Cover and leave to stand in the refrigerator for about 30 minutes.

2 Wash and stone the apricots, then replace the stone of each apricot with a cube of sugar. Bring plenty of salted water to the boil in a large saucepan.

3 On a lightly floured work surface, shape the dough into a roll, divide it into eight equal-sized pieces and press them flat. Wrap each apricot in a piece of dough, pressing the join firmly together, then shape them into dumplings.

4 Place the dumplings in the boiling water and simmer over low heat for about 10 minutes. Meanwhile, melt the butter in a frying pan until frothy, then fry the breadcrumbs in the butter over medium heat until golden-brown.

5 Remove the dumplings from the water with a slotted spoon and drain. Roll them in the buttery breadcrumbs, sprinkle with icing sugar, and serve.

Suggested accompaniment:
Marillensauce (Apricot sauce)
Cook 500 g stoned apricots in a saucepan with 100 g sugar, a little lemon juice and 12.5 cl water for about 12 minutes, until the apricots are soft, then press through a sieve.

Apricots

Native to China, apricots are cultivated in the warmer regions of Europe, as well as in Israel and California. In Lower Austria, extensive apricot orchards flourish across the Wachau region, the most beautiful stretch of the Danube.

The skin of the apricot, which has the texture of coarse velvet, is pale yellow to orange in colour, with a reddish blush where it has been exposed to the sun. The juicy sweet flesh can be white, yellow or orange and, when ripe, has a taste and a subtle fragrance similar to a peach.

Delicious raw and in fruit salads, apricots are also ideal for making compotes and jam; a large proportion of the fruit harvested in the Wachau is used for making apricot liqueur.

Apricots are often picked underripe, in order to survive transportation. Look for fruits with the warmest colour, and use them as soon as possible. They can be stored for a few days in the refrigerator.

Kaiserschmarren

Takes time • Lightly spiced

Fluffy pancake with plum compote

Serves 4

For the plum compote:
1 kg plums
1 unwaxed lemon
about 200 g caster sugar
5 cloves
1 cinnamon stick, about 2 cm long

For the pancake:
70 g raisins
1 tbsp rum
4 eggs
¼ litre milk
40 g caster sugar
160 g flour
salt
50 g butter
2 tbsp icing sugar

Preparation time: 2 hours

3,600 kg/860 calories per portion

1 Wash the plums, cut them in half and remove the stones. Wash the lemon thoroughly in hot water, thinly pare the rind and squeeze out the juice.

2 In a large saucepan, bring 12.5 cl water to the boil with the 200 g caster sugar, cloves, cinnamon stick, lemon rind and lemon juice. If the plums are very sour, add a little more sugar.

3 Keep the water on the boil for about 3 minutes, then discard the cloves, cinnamon and lemon rind. Add the plums and simmer over very low heat until the skins roll up and the plums have almost disintegrated. This takes about 1 hour. Stir the plums frequently while they are cooking, otherwise they will burn and stick to the pan. Leave the cooked plums to cool

4 To prepare the pancake, wash the raisins in hot water and pat dry. Put them in a bowl and sprinkle with rum.

5 Separate the eggs. Whisk together the milk, 40 g caster sugar and egg yolks in a separate bowl, then add the flour and mix to a smooth, thin batter. Whisk the egg whites with a little salt until stiff, then fold into the batter.

6 Heat the butter in a large frying pan, pour in the batter and fry for 1 to 2 minutes. Sprinkle the raisins over the batter. As soon as the underside is set, turn the pancake over. Continue to fry over low heat and, as it cooks, break the pancake into small pieces, using two forks. Once cooked, turn off the heat and leave to stand for 1 to 2 minutes, to allow the steam to escape.

7 Transfer the pancake to a warmed serving dish and sprinkle with the icing sugar. Serve at once, accompanied by a bowl of the plum compote, or, if you like, apple compote.

Variation: Topfenschmarren
(Fluffy quark pancake)
Whisk 250 g quark with 2 egg yolks and 2 tbsp soured cream. Add 70 g washed raisins, a little salt, 2 tbsp sugar and 1 tsp vanilla sugar (*see Note, page 96*) and the grated rind of ½ unwaxed lemon. Stir in 50 g flour. Whisk 2 egg whites until stiff, then carefully fold into the batter. Heat 40 g butter in a frying pan. Pour the batter into the pan and brown on both sides. While the pancake is cooking, break into small pieces, using two forks. Mix 2 tbsp caster sugar and 1 tsp ground cinnamon and sprinkle over the cooked pancake.

Note: To save time, make a larger quantity of plum compote, which will keep in the refrigerator for several days, so you have it ready the next time you want to make pancakes.

Apfelküchle

Easy • Vorarlberg

Apple fritters

2 eggs
150 g flour
salt
about ¼ litre milk
4 medium-sized apples
juice of 1 lemon
150 g clarified butter (see Glossary),
or 15 cl vegetable oil
3 tbsp caster sugar
1 tbsp ground cinnamon

Preparation time: 50 minutes

2,400 kJ/570 calories per portion

1 Separate the eggs. Sift the flour and a little salt into a bowl and make a well in the centre. Add the egg yolks and milk and beat well, gradually drawing in the flour to make a smooth batter. Leave to stand for about 15 minutes.

2 Peel the apples. Using an apple corer, remove the cores, then cut the apples into 1 cm-thick rings. Sprinkle the sliced apples with lemon juice to prevent them discolouring.

3 Whisk the egg whites until stiff, then carefully fold into the batter. Add a little more milk, if necessary.

4 Preheat the oven to its lowest setting. Heat the clarified butter or oil in a frying pan or deep fryer.

5 Coat the apple rings, three or four at a time, in the batter, then fry them in the fat over medium heat for about 5 minutes, until lightly browned, turning them once.

6 Keep the apple fritters warm in the oven until you have cooked them all. Mix the sugar and cinnamon together, sprinkle over the fritters, and serve immediately.

Suggested accompaniment:
Zimtsauce (Cinnamon sauce)
Whisk 2 egg yolks with 4 tbsp caster sugar until frothy. Add the pulp of 1 vanilla pod, 1 tbsp cinnamon, 1 tbsp cornflour and ½ litre milk. Cook slowly, stirring constantly, until the sauce is just below boiling point.

Apples

Apples are one of the most ancient and widespread fruits. Worldwide, there are more than 1,000 known species, and growers are constantly crossing different varieties to create new, differently flavoured types.

Excellent as a dessert fruit, apples are also frequently used in cooking, in both sweet and savoury dishes. Sweet apples, such as Golden Delicious or Cox's Orange Pippin, with their colourful skins, are ideal for fruit salads. For apple fritters, apple strudel and other warm desserts, use a tart variety, such as Jonathan, or the crisp green Granny Smith.

Since apples are a relatively hardy fruit, and easy to keep and store, they are readily available all year round. Look for unblemished fruit, and handle them carefully as they bruise easily. Apples will stay crisp longer if stored in the refrigerator.

Riebel

Easy • Vorarlberg **Semolina with raisins** *Serves 4*

½ *litre milk*

salt

200 g semolina

about 60 g butter

50 g raisins

2 tbsp caster sugar

Preparation time: 45 minutes

1,700 kJ/400 calories per portion

1 Heat the milk with a little salt in a saucepan. Trickle the semolina into the milk, stirring constantly, until the mixture comes away from the sides of the pan. This takes about 10 minutes.

2 Heat the butter in a large frying pan. Add the semolina and fry for 20 minutes, stirring frequently to make sure it does not stick to the pan, and chopping it into small pieces as it cooks. Add more butter, if necessary.

3 Wash the raisins, pat them dry, and add them to the semolina. Cook for a further 10 minutes. The *riebel* is ready when it is golden and crumbly.

4 Sprinkle with the sugar and serve, accompanied by fruit compote.

Variation:

Grießauflauf (Semolina pudding) Cool the cooked semolina. In a bowl, stir together 45 g butter, 2 tbsp icing sugar, 2 tsp vanilla sugar (*see Note, page 96*) and 2 egg yolks, until frothy, then stir in the semolina a spoonful at a time. Add 50 g washed raisins. Whisk 2 egg whites until stiff, then fold into the semolina mixture. Transfer to a buttered, floured baking dish and bake in centre of the oven at 200°C (400°F or Mark 6) for 30 minutes, until the top is golden-brown.

Schlosserbuben

Easy • Dinner-party dessert **Stuffed prunes in batter** *Serves 4*

24 large prunes

24 unskinned almonds

1 egg

120 g flour

12.5 cl light ale

1 tbsp vegetable oil

salt

1 tbsp caster sugar

clarified butter (see Glossary), or vegetable oil for deep-frying

70 g plain chocolate, finely grated

3 tbsp icing sugar

Preparation time: 40 minutes (plus 8 hours for soaking prunes)

2,400 kJ/570 calories per portion

1 Wash the prunes, place in a bowl, cover with lukewarm water and leave to soak for about 8 hours.

2 Stone the prunes. Bring a small saucepan of water to the boil, plunge the almonds briefly into the water, then peel them. Replace each prune stone with an almond.

3 Separate the egg. Mix the flour, light ale, 1 tbsp oil, egg yolk and a little salt to a smooth batter in a large bowl. Whisk the egg white with the sugar until stiff, then carefully fold it into the batter.

4 Heat a generous amount of clarified butter or oil in a large frying pan. If you are using an electric deep-fryer, preheat to 180°C (350°F).

5 Coat the prunes in the batter and fry in the hot fat over medium heat for about 5 minutes, until golden. Remove the prunes from the pan, drain them on paper towels and allow them to cool a little.

6 Mix the grated chocolate with the icing sugar. Toss the prunes in the chocolate mixture and serve at once, accompanied by a raspberry sauce, or vanilla custard (*recipe, page 100*).

Topfenpalatschinken

Quark-filled pancakes

For the batter:
100 g flour
about ¼ litre milk • 2 eggs
40 g caster sugar
salt
about 70 g butter

For the filling:
50 g raisins
1 tbsp rum
30 g softened butter
80 g caster sugar
grated rind of ½ unwaxed lemon
2 eggs
250 g quark

For the glaze and topping:
1 egg • 12.5 cl milk
1 tsp vanilla sugar (see Note, page 96)
2 tbsp icing sugar

Preparation time: 1½ hours

2,600 kJ/620 calories per portion

1 Mix the flour, 3 tbsp milk, 2 eggs, 40 g caster sugar and a little salt in a bowl to make a runny batter. Add a little more milk, if necessary.

2 Heat a frying pan and grease evenly with ½ tbsp butter. Using a ladle, pour about one eighth of the batter into the frying pan. Tilt the pan so that the batter covers the base, then cook over low heat until golden on both sides.

3 Repeat with the remaining batter to make eight pancakes. Pile the cooked pancakes on top of each other with greaseproof paper in between. If the batter becomes too thick, stir in a little more milk.

4 Preheat the oven to 200°C (400°F or Mark 6). Butter a shallow baking dish.

5 To make the filling, wash the raisins in hot water and pat dry. Place in a bowl and sprinkle with the rum. In a separate bowl, beat the butter, caster sugar and lemon rind until frothy. Separate the eggs and stir the yolks into the butter mixture. Stir in the quark and raisins. Whisk the egg whites until stiff, then fold them into the filling.

6 Spread the filling generously over the pancakes. Roll up the pancakes and cut them in half crosswise. Arrange the pancakes in the baking dish, overlapping them at an angle.

7 To make the glaze, whisk the egg, milk and vanilla sugar together in a bowl, then pour the mixture over the pancakes. Bake in the top of the oven for about 25 minutes, until golden.

8 Sprinkle the pancakes with icing sugar and serve at once, accompanied by vanilla custard (*recipe, page 100*).

Quark

This fresh, soft, slightly acidic curd cheese, with its delicate sour flavour, originated in central Europe and is especially popular in Germany. It is made from cow's milk, either whole fat, skimmed or with added extra cream. Local preferences and varying production techniques account for minor differences from country to country.

In Austria, quark (*Topfen*) is widely employed in cooking—for dumplings, pastries and strudels. It can be eaten on its own or as an accompaniment to fresh fruit, salads and vegetables. It is delicious mixed with herbs or spices.

Several different varieties of quark are available in Austria, ranging from very low fat (less than 10 per cent) to double cream fat content. In the UK, the most widely available type is low-fat quark, which has a fat content of 2 to 3 per cent. It can be bought in most large supermarkets.

Salzburger Nockerln
Soufflé with icing sugar

Quick and easy • Salzburg

Serves 4

3 egg yolks
6 egg whites
salt
3 tbsp caster sugar
2 tsp vanilla sugar (see Note, page 96)
20 g flour
grated rind of ½ unwaxed lemon
20 g butter
4 tbsp milk
2 tbsp icing sugar

Preparation time: 30 minutes

850 kJ/200 calories per portion

1 Preheat the oven to 225°C (425°F or Mark 7). Whisk the egg yolks in a bowl. In a separate bowl, whisk the egg whites with a little salt until stiff, gradually adding the sugars.

2 Carefully fold about a third of the beaten egg white into the egg yolks, then fold this mixture into the rest of the egg white. Sift the flour and fold it carefully into the egg mixture with the grated lemon rind.

3 Put the butter and milk in a 3 litre, shallow, fireproof baking dish and bring to the boil on top of the cooker.

4 Transfer the soufflé mixture to the baking dish, using a spatula to shape it into three large mounds.

5 Bake in the centre of the oven for about 10 minutes, until the top is golden-brown. Do not open the oven while the soufflé is cooking. The soufflé should still be creamy inside.

6 Sprinkle with the icing sugar and serve immediately.

Note: This feather-light soufflé must be served straight away, otherwise it will collapse. It may also sink if it is caught in a draught or if you handle the dish too roughly.

Topfennockerln
Quark dumplings with strawberry sauce

Takes time • Sophisticated

Serves 4

50 g softened butter
2 eggs • 250 g quark
130 g fresh breadcrumbs
100 g flour
3 tbsp caster sugar • salt
300 g fresh strawberries
1 tbsp lemon juice
5 tbsp icing sugar
50 g butter
strawberry leaves for decoration

*Preparation time: 45 minutes
(plus 30 minutes' standing time)*

2,700 kJ/640 calories per portion

1 Beat the softened butter and the eggs in a bowl until frothy, then stir in the quark, 50 g breadcrumbs, the flour, sugar and a little salt. Cover the dough and leave to stand in the refrigerator for about 30 minutes.

2 Bring plenty of water to the boil in a large saucepan. Using a tablespoon, shape the dough into small dumplings. Add them to the boiling water and cook over low heat for about 15 minutes. The dumplings will float to the surface when they are cooked.

3 Meanwhile, wash the strawberries, then purée them in a blender with the lemon juice and 3 tbsp icing sugar.

4 Heat the remaining 50 g butter in a frying pan until it froths, then add the remaining breadcrumbs and stir-fry over medium heat until golden-brown. Remove the dumplings from the water with a slotted spoon, drain thoroughly, then coat them in the breadcrumbs.

5 Spoon the sauce onto four individual plates. Arrange the dumplings on top, sprinkle with the remaining icing sugar and decorate with strawberry leaves.

Scheiterhaufen

Easy • Family pudding **Apple meringue pudding** *Serves 8*

4 day-old bread rolls
¼ litre milk
2 eggs
80 g caster sugar
2 tsp vanilla sugar (see Note, page 96)
50 g raisins
50 g butter, straight from the refrigerator
500 g tart eating apples
50 g chopped almonds
½ tsp ground cinnamon
2 egg whites

Preparation time: 30 minutes (plus 50 minutes' baking time)

1,250 kJ/300 calories per portion

1 Thinly slice the bread rolls. Whisk the milk in a bowl with the eggs, 40 g caster sugar and the vanilla sugar. Wash the raisins and spread them on paper towels to dry. Cut the cold butter into slivers. Butter a baking dish.

2 Preheat the oven to 200°C (400°F or Mark 6). Peel, quarter and core the apples, then slice them thinly.

3 Layer half the sliced bread rolls in the bottom of the baking dish. Pour half the egg and milk mixture over the top.

4 Arrange the apple slices over the bread, then sprinkle the raisins, almonds and cinnamon over the top. Cover with the rest of the bread, then pour over the remaining egg and milk mixture. Dot with the slivers of butter.

5 Bake in the centre of the oven for about 40 minutes, until the top is a light golden colour.

6 Towards the end of the cooking time, whisk the egg whites until stiff. Whisk in half the remaining sugar, then carefully fold in the rest.

7 Turn up the oven to 220°C (425°F or Mark 7). Spread the meringue on top of the pudding. Bake in the top of the oven for about 10 minutes, until the meringue is golden-brown.

Variations: Kipfelkoch
(Croissant and apple pudding)
Instead of bread rolls, use croissants and omit the vanilla sugar, almonds and meringue. Prepare the pudding to the end of Step 4 and bake in the oven at 200°C (400°F or Mark 6) for about 45 minutes, until golden. The pudding should be crisp on top. Serve sprinkled with 2 tbsp icing sugar.

Salzburger Koch
(Salzburg pudding)
Soak 4 day-old bread rolls in 12.5 cl milk, then squeeze thoroughly and mince in a food processor. Mix 80 g butter, 3 tbsp icing sugar and 2 tbsp vanilla sugar until frothy. Gradually stir in 3 egg yolks. Add 50 g chopped almonds and the minced bread rolls. Whisk 3 egg whites until stiff, whisk in 1 tbsp caster sugar, then fold into the mixture. Butter a baking dish and line with breadcrumbs. Transfer half the pudding mixture to the baking dish. Top with 300 g stoned cherries or sliced apples. Cover with the rest of the pudding mixture. Bake in the centre of a preheated oven at 200°C (400°F or Mark 6) for about 40 minutes, until golden.

Note: Cinnamon is produced from the inner bark of the young branches of the cinnamon tree. It is sold in sticks or ground to a powder. Ground cinnamon is mainly used as a flavouring for cakes, pastries and desserts, while cinnamon sticks are added to compotes, sauces for serving with game, and mulled wine.

NATÜRLICH
STREU
ZUCKER

NATÜRLI
STRE
ZUCKER

Das si...Telefon
022/15 6...
hier erhal...
un...

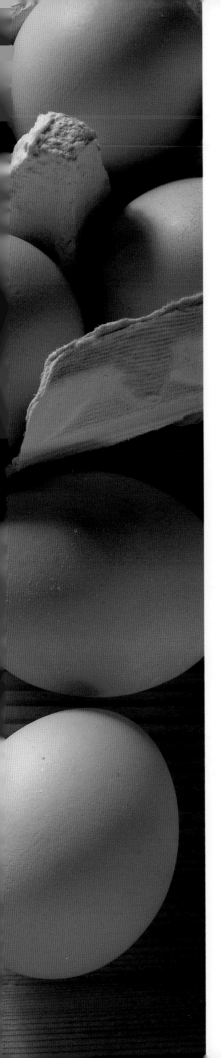

FANCY CAKES
AND BISCUITS

Baking is one of the most
enjoyable of culinary skills—
who can resist the smell of a
freshly baked cake or home-made
biscuits?—and one at which Austria's
cooks have always excelled.

This chapter contains a selection
of recipes that have found fame far
beyond the borders of Austria: the
rich, moist *Sachertorte*, for example,
created in 1832 by a master sugar
baker whose descendants for many
years ran Vienna's renowned Hotel
Sacher. Or *Faschingskrapfen*, an even
older Viennese speciality invented as
long ago as 1615. These fluffy, sugary
doughnut-like treats are particularly
delicious when freshly prepared.

Many of the more luxurious cakes
are simpler to make than you might
imagine; the fluted *Kaisergugelhupf*
and the delicately latticed *Linzer Torte*
can be mastered with a little time and
patience. Accompanied by a cup of
freshly ground coffee, or refreshing
tea, they provide a touch of luxury at
any time of the day—especially when
that typically Viennese speciality,
whipped cream, is added! For a
simpler treat, there is the inexpensive
Reindling, or the smaller biscuits and
cakes such as *Ischler Törtchen* or
Vanillekipferln.

Kaisergugelhupf

Almond gugelhupf

300 g flour
20 g fresh, or 2 tsp dried, yeast
70 g caster sugar
about 12.5 cl lukewarm milk
50 g raisins
1 tbsp rum
80 g softened butter
2 tsp vanilla sugar (see Note, page 96)
4 egg yolks
grated rind of ½ unwaxed lemon
salt
about 15 almonds
2 tbsp icing sugar

Preparation time: 1¼ hours (plus 1 hour for proving)

930 kJ/220 calories per slice

1 All the dough ingredients must be at warm room temperature.

2 Sift the flour into a large bowl and make a well in the middle. Crumble the fresh yeast into the well. Add 1 tsp sugar and a little lukewarm milk to the yeast and stir well, then sprinkle with a little flour from around the edge. Cover and leave in a warm place until cracks can be seen in the flour. This takes about 15 minutes. If using dried yeast, sprinkle it into a little milk with the 1 tsp sugar and leave until frothy.

3 Wash the raisins, pat dry, then put in a bowl and sprinkle with the rum.

4 Beat the butter with the rest of the caster sugar and the vanilla sugar until frothy. Gradually add the egg yolks, lemon rind and a little salt.

5 Add the butter and egg mixture to the dough. Stir with the flour to make a smooth, fluffy dough, adding a little more milk, if necessary. Cover the dough and leave to rise for about 25 minutes, until it has doubled in size.

6 Grease a 22 cm *gugelhupf* mould with butter and sprinkle with flour. Shake off any excess flour. Bring a small saucepan of water to the boil, dip the almonds into the boiling water,

then peel and halve them. Spread them evenly over the base of the mould.

7 Briefly knead the dough and stir in the raisins. Place the dough in the mould. Smooth the surface, cover the mould and leave to prove for 25 minutes. Meanwhile, preheat the oven to 200°C (400°F or Mark 6).

8 Bake the *gugelhupf* on the bottom shelf of the oven for about 45 minutes, until a fine skewer inserted into the thickest part comes out clean.

9 Turn out the *gugelhupf* onto a wire cooling rack and leave to cool. Sprinkle with icing sugar and serve.

Variation:
Altwiener Patzerlgugelhupf

(*Gugelhupf* with nut and raisin filling) Omit the raisins and rum. When the dough has risen for the first time, roll it out to the thickness of a finger, then divide it into three strips. To make the filling for the first strip, bring 2 tbsp milk to the boil and add 50 g poppy seeds, 1 tbsp sugar, 1 tbsp fresh breadcrumbs and a tiny amount of honey and ground cinnamon. Cook briefly, then stir in 1 tbsp raisins. Spread this mixture over the first strip of pastry. Prepare the filling for the second strip, using finely ground walnuts instead of poppy seeds. For the third filling, mix 50 g quark,

15 g butter, 1 tsp icing sugar, 1 tsp cornflour, a little cinnamon and grated lemon rind, a few drops of lemon juice and 1 tbsp raisins. Roll up each strip of dough, then arrange the three rolls, one on top of the other, in the mould. Leave to prove for about 30 minutes, then bake on the bottom shelf of a preheated oven (200°C (400°F or Mark 6)), for about 45 minutes.

Reindling
Nut and raisin roll

For the dough:
500 g flour
30 g fresh, or 1 tbsp dried, yeast
30 g caster sugar
about ¼ litre lukewarm milk
80 g butter
1 egg
2 egg yolks
grated rind of ½ unwaxed lemon
salt

For the filling:
100 g raisins
1 tbsp rum
30 g butter
100 g sugar
1 tbsp ground cinnamon
100 g finely chopped walnuts
2 tbsp icing sugar

Preparation time: 1½ hours
(plus 1 hour for proving)

1,600 kJ/380 calories per slice

1 All the dough ingredients must be at warm room temperature.

2 Sift the flour into a large bowl and make a well in the middle. Crumble the fresh yeast into the well. Add 1 tsp caster sugar and a little lukewarm milk to the yeast and stir well, then sprinkle with a little flour from around the edge. Cover and leave in a warm place until cracks can be seen in the flour. This takes about 15 minutes. If using dried yeast, sprinkle it into a little milk with the 1 tsp caster sugar and leave until frothy.

3 Melt the butter and the remaining sugar in the rest of the warm milk. Add the egg, egg yolks, lemon rind and a little salt and mix thoroughly.

4 Add the mixture to the dough, stir in the flour and knead to a smooth dough. Add a little more milk, if necessary. The dough should be bubbly and come away easily from the side of the bowl. Cover and leave to prove for 25 minutes.

5 Wash the raisins, pat dry, then put them in a bowl and sprinkle with the rum. Butter a 23 cm round cake tin.

6 Briefly knead the dough again, then, on a lightly floured surface, roll it out to a 25 by 40 cm rectangle.

7 To make the filling, melt the butter in a frying pan. Mix the sugar and cinnamon together on a plate.

8 Drizzle the dough with the melted butter, and sprinkle over the chopped walnuts, raisins, and the cinnamon and sugar mixture.

9 Shape the dough into a roll about 40 cm long, then curl it into a spiral and place in the buttered tin (*below*). Cover the dough with a clean tea towel and leave to prove for 25 minutes.

10 Meanwhile, preheat the oven to 200°C (400°F or Mark 6).

11 Bake on the bottom shelf of the oven for about 45 minutes, until a fine skewer inserted into the centre comes out clean.

12 Remove the cooked cake from the tin and leave to cool on a wire rack. Serve, sprinkled with icing sugar.

Tiroler Kletzenbrot

Easy • Tyrol **Fruit loaf** *Makes 2 loaves (about 40 slices)*

300 g dried pears
200 g stoned prunes
40 g fresh, or 4 tsp dried, yeast
50 g caster sugar
500 g rye flour
salt
200 g dried figs
100 g hazelnuts
100 g walnuts
100 g raisins • 100 g currants
50 g candied lemon peel
50 g candied orange peel
1 tsp ground cinnamon
1 tsp ground cloves
allspice
2 tbsp rum
juice and finely grated rind of
1 unwaxed lemon
2 tbsp black coffee

Preparation time: about 2 hours
(plus 1¾ hours for proving)

570 kJ/140 calories per slice

1 Place the dried pears and prunes in a large saucepan with enough water to cover, then cook for about 10 minutes, until soft. Drain and reserve the water.

2 Mix the yeast with 1 tsp caster sugar, 2 tbsp rye flour and 12.5 cl lukewarm water and leave for about 15 minutes.

3 Measure the cooking liquid and, if necessary, top up with enough cold water to make it up to ¼ litre. Pour it into a large bowl. Stir in the yeast dough and the remaining sugar and a little salt. Stir in the remaining rye flour. Using the dough hook in a food

processor, work the mixture to a smooth dough. If the dough is too firm, add a little more water a spoonful at a time. Cover the dough and leave in a warm place to rise for about 60 minutes.

4 Cut the pears, first into slices, then into wide strips, removing the stalks and cores. Cut the prunes and figs into thick strips. Coarsely chop the hazelnuts and walnuts. Wash the raisins and currants. Chop the candied lemon and orange peel into small dice. Mix all the fruit and nuts together, and season with the cinnamon, ground cloves, a small amount of allspice, the rum, lemon juice and lemon rind.

5 Knead the dough and the fruit mixture together and shape it into two loaves. With damp hands, smooth the tops of the loaves, then leave to prove for 30 minutes.

6 Preheat the oven to 200°C (400°F or Mark 6). Line a baking sheet with baking parchment or greaseproof paper. Bring some water to the boil and pour it into a shallow ovenproof bowl.

7 Brush the fruit loaves with the coffee and place them on the baking sheet. Stand the bowl of boiling water in the bottom of the oven.

8 Bake the loaves in the centre of the oven for about 1 hour 10 minutes, splashing them with water from time to time.

9 Leave the loaves for at least two days before slicing. They will keep for up to three months, but are at their best after about a week.

Note: Dried fruits are produced by removing the water from fully ripened fresh fruit by evaporation. The picked fruit is either dried naturally or in dehydration units—which blast it with hot air—and the moisture content reduced to about 20 per cent, the critical limit for the growth of fungi and bacteria. The dried fruit will then keep for months.

Dried fruits are especially nourishing because the nutrients in the fresh fruit become highly concentrated when they are dried. They can be eaten raw as a snack, or cooked in sweet and savoury dishes, desserts, cakes and biscuits.

Sachertorte

Chocolate cake

For the cake:
130 g plain cooking chocolate
6 eggs
130 g softened butter
100 g icing sugar
2 tsp vanilla sugar (see Note, page 96)
100 g caster sugar
130 g flour
about 4 tbsp apricot jam

For the icing:
250 g plain cooking chocolate
300 g sugar

To accompany:
17.5 cl whipped cream

Preparation time: 2½ hours (plus a total of 20 hours' standing time)

2,500 kJ/600 calories per portion

1 Melt the 130 g cooking chocolate in the top of a double saucepan or a heatproof bowl set over a saucepan of hot water; or use a microwave (*see Note*).

2 Preheat the oven to 180°C (350°F or Mark 4). Line a 23 cm round cake tin with baking parchment or greaseproof paper.

3 Separate the eggs. Beat the butter, icing sugar and vanilla sugar in a bowl until frothy. Gradually stir in the egg yolks and melted chocolate. Whisk the egg whites and caster sugar, but do not let the mixture become too stiff. Fold the egg whites into the chocolate. Sift the flour over the mixture and quickly and lightly blend it in.

4 Transfer the mixture to the cake tin, smooth the top and bake in the centre of the oven for about 1 hour. The cake is done when it gives slightly if you press it with your finger, but no fingerprint is left.

5 Leave the cake in the tin until it is completely cool. Use a sharp knife to loosen the cake from the sides of the tin. Turn the cake out and remove the baking parchment or greaseproof paper. Slice off the top of the cake to create a flat surface, if wished.

6 Melt the apricot jam in a small saucepan and spread it thinly over the cake. Leave the cake to stand in a cool place for a few hours, preferably overnight, before icing.

7 To make the icing, break the chocolate into pieces and put in a small saucepan with the sugar and 12.5 cl water. Bring to the boil, stirring constantly, and continue cooking over low heat for 5 minutes, stirring, until the mixture begins to thicken. Remove from the heat.

8 Using the back of a spoon or a wooden spatula, stir the mixture back and forth against the sides of the pan until it reaches a consistency suitable for icing. While stirring, scrape the mixture from the sides of the pan and blend in. The icing should be thick, shiny and lukewarm. If it becomes too cool or too thick, reheat over low heat or add a few drops of water.

9 Pour the chocolate icing over the cake all at once. Using a palette knife, spread it evenly and fairly thickly over the top and sides. Transfer the cake to a serving plate and leave to stand for several hours.

10 Using a knife dipped in hot water, cut the *sachertorte* into 12 slices. Serve on dessert plates, accompanied by the whipped cream.

Note: To melt chocolate in the microwave, break it into small pieces and cook on low just until the chocolate is soft and looks glossy on top. Remove from the microwave and stir until melted. The melting times vary according to the container used, so check every minute during melting. Do not melt on high or the chocolate may scorch.

Linzer Torte

Latticed redcurrant jam tart

150 g flour
200 g ground almonds
100 g caster sugar
1 tsp ground cinnamon
ground cloves
grated rind of ½ unwaxed lemon
salt
2 egg yolks
150 g butter, straight from the refrigerator
200 g redcurrant jam
50 g flaked almonds
1 tbsp icing sugar

Preparation time: 1½ hours
(plus 30 minutes' standing time and 30 minutes' cooling time)

1,500 kJ/360 calories per slice

1 Mix the flour, ground almonds, sugar, cinnamon, ground cloves, lemon rind and a little salt together in a heap on a work surface. Make a well in the middle and place 1 egg yolk in the well.

2 Sliver the butter around the edge of the heap and, working inwards, blend to a smooth dough. Put in a bowl, cover and leave to stand in the refrigerator for about 30 minutes. Preheat the oven to 180°C (350°F or Mark 4).

3 Butter a 23 cm round cake tin. Place about two-thirds of the dough in the tin, patting it out evenly to cover the base. Spread the redcurrant jam on top, leaving a border about the width of a finger.

4 Divide the remaining dough in half. Take one half and roll it into pencil-thick rolls. Arrange the rolls in an evenly-spaced lattice pattern on top of the jam (*above*).

5 Shape the rest of the pastry into a slightly thicker roll and arrange it around the edge of the tart (*above*). Press the pastry border gently downwards. Brush the border and the lattice with the remaining egg yolk.

6 Sprinkle the tart with the flaked almonds and bake in the centre of the oven for about 45 minutes, until lightly browned. Leave to cool thoroughly, then sprinkle with icing sugar.

Note: Cloves are the dried buds of the evergreen clove tree, which grows to a height of about 12 metres. The best cloves come from the Moluccas, formerly called the Spice Islands, in Indonesia, but those from Zanzibar and Madagascar are also good. Shaped like nails, reddish-brown cloves have a sweetish aroma and a piquant flavour. Whole cloves are used to add flavour to fish and roast meat, as well as for preserving fruit, and as an ingredient in mulled wine and punch. Ground cloves are widely used for cakes and pastries, especially in Christmas fare.

Burgenländische Mohntorte

Easy • Burgenland — **Flourless poppy-seed cake**

4 eggs
125 g butter
100 g, plus 2 tbsp, icing sugar
50 g candied lemon peel
50 g caster sugar
150 g ground poppy seeds (see opposite)

Preparation time: 1½ hours

1,300 kJ/310 calories per slice

1 Separate the eggs. Beat the butter, 100 g icing sugar and egg yolks in a bowl until frothy. Chop the candied lemon peel into small dice and add to the mixture. Whisk the egg whites until stiff. Add the sugar and continue to whisk until very stiff. Gradually fold the beaten egg whites and poppy seeds into the butter mixture.

2 Preheat the oven to 180°C (350°F or Mark 4). Butter a 23 cm cake tin and sprinkle the inside with flour.

3 Transfer the mixture to the tin, smooth the top and bake in the centre of the oven for 1 hour.

4 Leave the cake in the tin until completely cool. Turn out and sprinkle with the remaining icing sugar, using, if you like, a paper template or doily to create a pattern across the top.

Variation: Allow the cake to cool thoroughly, then slice horizontally through the middle and sandwich the two halves together with redcurrant jam. Mix 200 g icing sugar and the juice of 1 lemon to make a smooth glacé icing and use this to ice the cake, instead of sprinkling it with the icing sugar.

Poppy seeds

These small, blueish-black non-narcotic seeds are harvested from the opium poppy, which is cultivated in China, India, Iran, Turkey and in the Waldviertel in Lower Austria. The most common European variety is the black poppy seed, although cream-coloured ones are also available. In their natural state, they are almost odourless and flavourless, acquiring their "nutty" flavour when toasted or baked.

Poppy seeds are a popular ingredient in Jewish and Indian cookery—added to curries, for example—but they are most commonly sprinkled over breads, or used as a filling for cakes and pastries. They make a decorative addition to vegetable dips, spreads and salads, or sprinkled over cooked potatoes, chilled soups and savoury pie crusts.

Poppy seeds are usually sold whole. Small amounts can be crushed with a pestle and mortar or rolling pin; larger quantities can be ground in a blender or coffee mill.

Faschingskrapfen

Apricot jam doughnuts

Makes about 12 doughnuts

300 g flour
20 g fresh, or 2 tsp dried, yeast
3 tbsp caster sugar
about 12.5 cl lukewarm milk
60 g butter
1 tsp vanilla sugar (see Note, page 96)
3 egg yolks
grated rind of ½ unwaxed lemon
salt
vegetable oil for deep-frying
150 g apricot jam
4 tbsp icing sugar

Preparation time: 1 hour (plus 1 hour for cooling)

1,200 kJ/290 calories per doughnut

1 All the dough ingredients must be at warm room temperature.

2 Sift the flour into a large bowl and make a well in the middle. Crumble the fresh yeast into the well. Add 1 tsp caster sugar and a little lukewarm milk to the yeast and stir well, then sprinkle with a little flour from around the edge. Cover and leave in a warm place until cracks can be seen in the flour. This takes about 15 minutes. If using dried yeast, sprinkle it into a little of the lukewarm milk with the 1 tsp sugar and leave until frothy.

3 Melt the butter in a small saucepan. Dissolve the remaining caster sugar and the vanilla sugar in the rest of the warm milk and add the egg yolks, grated lemon rind and a little salt. Mix thoroughly. Add all these ingredients to the yeast mixture and stir to a smooth dough with the flour. If necessary, add a little warm milk. Cover the dough and leave to rise for about 20 minutes.

4 Divide the dough into about 12 pieces. On a lightly floured surface, with floured hands, roll the pieces into small balls. When all the doughnuts are ready, press them gently to flatten them a little. Cover with a clean tea towel and leave to prove for 20 minutes.

5 Heat a generous amount of oil in a deep frying pan. If using a deep-fryer, preheat it to 175° (350°F). Place the doughnuts, in batches, in the hot fat, with the topside facing downwards. Cover the pan and fry the doughnuts for about 3 minutes, then turn them,

preferably with wooden chopsticks. Fry for a further 4 minutes, until golden-brown with a pale strip round the middle. Place the doughnuts on a wire rack to drain, and leave to cool.

6 Place the apricot jam in an icing bag fitted with a thin nozzle. When the doughnuts are cool, insert the nozzle into the pale central strip and squeeze a little jam into the middle (*below*).

7 Leave the doughnuts until completely cold. Serve the same day, sprinkled with icing sugar.

Variation: Mix 150 g icing sugar with 3 tbsp lemon juice and then ice the doughnuts while still warm. Allow the icing to set before serving.

Zaunerstollen

Easy • Chilled cake **Chocolate log**

Makes about 10 slices

120 g ground almonds
120 g Amaretti biscuits
250 g plain chocolate
25 cl whipping cream
almond oil or butter

For the icing:
100 g plain chocolate
80 g butter

Preparation time: 45 minutes
(plus 2 hours for chilling)

1,500 kJ/360 calories per slice

1 In a dry frying pan, toast the ground almonds for a few minutes, until lightly golden. Place the Amaretti biscuits in a deep bowl and crush them finely with a fork.

2 Break the chocolate into pieces and melt it in the top of a double saucepan or a heatproof bowl set over a saucepan. Add the cream, a little at a time, and stir until the mixture is smooth and thick. Allow the chocolate cream to cool slightly, then stir in the almonds and biscuit crumbs.

3 Brush a 29 cm-long, fluted, cylindrical mould or tin with almond oil or melted butter.

4 Pour the mixture into the mould, smooth the top, then chill it in the refrigerator for about 2 hours.

5 Turn the log out of the mould. To make the icing, break the chocolate into the top of a double saucepan or a heatproof bowl set over a saucepan of hot water. Add the butter and 1 tbsp water and stir until the chocolate has melted. Pour the icing over the cake and leave to set.

Ischler Törtchen

Easy • Teatime treat

Apricot biscuits

Makes about 20 biscuits

250 g flour
150 g finely ground almonds
120 g caster sugar
2 tsp vanilla sugar (see Note, page 96)
ground cinnamon • salt
250 g butter, straight from the refrigerator
about 150 g apricot jam

For the icing:
60 g plain chocolate
45 g butter
30 g finely chopped pistachio nuts

Preparation time: 2 hours

1,100 kJ/260 calories per biscuit

1 Sift the flour onto a work surface. Add the almonds, caster sugar, vanilla sugar and a little ground cinnamon and salt. Cut the butter into slivers and add to the flour, then quickly knead all the ingredients to a smooth dough. Leave the dough to stand in the refrigerator for about 30 minutes.

2 Preheat the oven to 200°C (400°F or Mark 6). Line a baking sheet with greaseproof paper.

3 On a lightly floured surface, roll out the pastry until it is about 3 mm thick. Using a glass about 5 cm in diameter, cut the pastry into circles. Arrange the pastry circles on the baking sheet and

bake in the centre of the oven for about 12 minutes, until golden.

4 Remove the biscuits from the baking sheet and leave to cool completely. When cool, spread half the circles with apricot jam and place the remaining biscuits on top.

5 To make the icing, break the chocolate into the top of a double saucepan or a heatproof bowl set over a saucepan of hot water. Add the butter and 2 to 3 tsp water and stir until the chocolate has melted. Spread the icing over the biscuits, then sprinkle them with chopped pistachio nuts and leave to cool completely.

Vanillekipferln

Vanilla mini croissants

250 g flour
200 g ground almonds
150 g icing sugar
salt
200 g butter, straight from the refrigerator
4 tsp vanilla sugar (see Note, page 96)

Preparation time: 1½ hours (plus 1 hour's standing time)

440 kJ/100 calories per croissant

1 Sift the flour onto a work surface, and add the almonds. Stir in 50 g icing sugar and a little salt. Cut the butter into slivers and add to the dry ingredients. Quickly work all the ingredients to a smooth dough.

2 Cover the dough and leave to stand in the refrigerator for about 1 hour. Meanwhile, preheat the oven to 180°C (350°F or Mark 4).

3 On a lightly floured surface, shape the dough into several rolls about 2 cm in diameter. Cut the rolls of pastry into pieces about the thickness of a finger (you should have about 40 pieces). Shape the pieces into small sausage shapes about 6 cm long, pointed at either end, then bend them into a crescent shape. Arrange them on an ungreased baking sheet and bake in the centre of the oven for about 15 minutes, until lightly browned.

4 Mix the remaining icing sugar with the vanilla sugar. While the croissants are still hot, carefully coat them in the sugar mixture. Serve warm or cold.

Variation: Klosterkipferln

(Chocolate croissants)
Add 50 g finely grated plain chocolate and 1 egg to the dough. Instead of coating the baked croissants in vanilla sugar, melt 100 g plain chocolate in the top of a double saucepan or a heatproof bowl set over a saucepan of hot water, then dip each end of the cooled croissants in the chocolate. Leave to dry on a wire rack.

Butter

Butter is a versatile fat. It makes an excellent tasty spread on bread and savoury biscuits; it is an essential ingredient in baking, giving a rich, distinctive flavour to cakes, biscuits and sweet pastries; and it is used in many classic sauces. It has a very high fat content—about 80 per cent—and is rich in vitamin A.

Made by churning fresh cream, butter varies in colour and flavour from country to country, and from region to region within a country, depending on the richness of the grass, or the amount of salt—added as a preservative—that it contains.

Slightly salted butter is the most popular and most widely available type and is suitable for all methods of cooking and baking—though unsalted butter is particularly good for pastry.

Store butter in the refrigerator or in a cool dark place, wrapped or well covered to prevent it from picking up the flavours of other foods. It can be stored for two to three weeks, or up until the "best before" date displayed on the wrapper.

Suggested Menus

The Austrians eat well, and often. A typical meal generally consists of soup, meat with side dishes—especially potatoes—and the obligatory rich dessert. Sometimes, a substantial main course is complemented by vegetables, salad and fruit. Austrians also like to serve a hot pudding as a combined main course and dessert, perhaps preceded by a hearty soup. Crusty bread is always a welcome accompaniment, as are simple green salads. This selection of menus, put together from recipes featured in the book, contains suggested menus for every occasion, from quick and simple everyday meals to more elaborate feasts. Items which you can easily buy or make yourself, and for which recipes are not provided, are marked with an asterisk.

Quick menus

Clear soup with shredded pancake	24
Beef escalopes with onion rings	54
Fresh fruit*	—
Wine soup with cinnamon croûtons	32
Chanterelles in cream sauce	84
Cheese board*	—
Clear soup with bread and bacon dumplings	27
Calf's kidneys with soured cream	45
Green salad*	—
Cheese and grapes*	—
Beer soup	32
Chicken fried in breadcrumbs	72
Cucumber salad*	—
Sorbet*	—

Economical menus

Vegetable soup*	—
Potato dumplings with poppy-seed butter	102
Fruit salad*	—
Cauliflower in batter	38
Little sauerkraut pies	80
Mixed salad*	—
Semolina with raisins	110
Peach compote*	—
Cream of pumpkin soup	30
Fried potatoes with pork or ham	82
Endive salad*	—
Apple compote*	—
Clear soup with liver dumplings	26
Quark-filled pasta pockets	78
Lettuce salad*	—
Fresh fruit*	—

Beef broth with soured cream and caraway seeds	33
Potato and bacon goulash	84
Rhubarb compote*	—
Clear soup with shredded pancake	24
Fried potatoes with salt cod	82
Chinese cabbage salad*	—
Apple and raisin strudel	94
Clear soup with bread and bacon dumplings	27
Yeast dumplings with vanilla custard	100
Fresh fruit*	—
Clear soup with liver dumplings	26
Pasta squares baked with cabbage	77
Lettuce salad*	—
Apple purée*	—
Potato and mushroom soup	34
Yeast dumplings with poppy seeds	98
Fresh fruit*	—

Menus to prepare in advance

Clear soup with shredded pancake	24
Veal and onion goulash	56
Fruit salad*	—
Mixed green salad*	—
Potato and bacon goulash	84
Apple and raisin strudel	94
Vegetable platter*	—
Pasta squares baked with ham	76
Green salad*	—
Sorbet*	—

Family menus

Clear soup with shredded pancake	24
Stuffed peppers	90
Mixed berry compote*	—
Clear soup with semolina dumplings	24
Veal rissoles with puréed potatoes	60
Green salad*	—
Fruit and ice cream*	—
Vegetable soup	—
Pasta squares baked with ham	76
Green salad*	—
Quark dumplings with strawberry sauce	114
Cauliflower in batter	38
Apple meringue pudding	116
Orange salad*	—

Sunday classics

Clear soup with shredded pancake	24
Veal escalopes fried in breadcrumbs	56
Potato salad and cucumber salad*	—
Apple and raisin strudel	94
Clear soup with semolina dumplings	24
Chicken fried in breadcrumbs	72
Rice and salad*	—
Quark strudel	96
Hot vanilla custard	100
Clear soup with liver dumplings	26
Breast of veal with mushroom stuffing	58
Rice, peas and salad*	—
Apple fritters, served with cinnamon sauce	108
Clear soup with shredded pancake	24
Boiled beef	52
Apple and horseradish sauce, or chive sauce	53
Fruit and ice cream*	—
Cream of pumpkin soup	30
Roast pork with potato dumplings	64
Coleslaw*	—
Fresh fruit*	—

Dinner party menus

Wine soup with cinnamon croûtons	32
Roast goose with chestnut and apple stuffing	73
Red cabbage with apple*	—
Quark dumplings with strawberry sauce	114
Cream of pumpkin soup	30
Trout fillets with mushroom sauce	68
Parsley potatoes*	—
Quark strudel	96
Asparagus with toasted breadcrumbs	40
Beef escalopes with onion rings	54
Croquette potatoes*	—
Stuffed prunes in batter	110
Raspberry purée*	—

An Austrian buffet

Beef salad with eggs and peppers	48
Black bread*	—
Croissants with ham filling	46
Chicken fried in breadcrumbs	72
Potato salad*	—
Cucumber salad*	—

Veal and onion goulash	56
Fresh white baguettes*	—
White cabbage strudel	88
Cheeseboard*	—
Quark strudel	96
Apricot biscuits	135
Fresh fruit*	—
Coffee and whipped cream*	—

Spring menus

Asparagus with toasted breadcrumbs	40
Trout fillets with mushroom sauce	68
New potatoes*	—
Quark dumplings with strawberry sauce	114
Beef broth with soured cream and caraway seeds	33
Pasta pockets with spinach filling	78
Mixed green salad*	—
Fresh strawberries*	—

Summer menus

Cauliflower cheese	38
Chanterelles in cream sauce	84
Apricot dumplings in buttery breadcrumbs	104
Cauliflower in batter	38
Stuffed peppers	90
Parsley potatoes*	—
Selection of summer fruits*	—

Autumn menus

Cream of pumpkin soup	30
Roast goose with chestnut and apple stuffing	73
Red cabbage with apple*	—
Apple and raisin strudel	94
Wine soup (make the croûtons without cinnamon)	32
Stuffed cabbage rolls	86
Boiled potatoes*	—
Apple fritters, served with cinnamon sauce	108

Winter menu

Potato and mushroom soup	34
Carp fillet with horseradish	68
Stuffed prunes in batter	110
Vanilla custard	100

Glossary

This Glossary is intended as a brief guide to some less familiar cookery terms and ingredients, including words or items found on Austrian menus.

Alter: mature wine more than a year old, the opposite of *Heuriger*.

Aniseed: seeds of the anise plant, native to the Mediterranean region, and widely used in baking for such specialities as *Anisbrot, Anisscharten* and *Anisbögen*.

Backerbsen: pea-sized pieces of dough fried in fat and added to soups.

Bauernkrapfen: flat, round, plate-sized yeast cake that is deep-fried.

Bauernschmaus: hearty meal of roast pork, *Geselchtes* (smoked pork), Vienna sausage, dumpling and sauerkraut.

Beisel (*Beisl*): little inn serving simple, inexpensive food.

Beugel: a croissant-shaped pastry filled with poppy seeds or nuts.

Beuschel: calf's or pig's lungs and heart (*Salonbeuschel, recipe page 62*).

Brauner (large or small): black coffee with milk.

Brettljause: cuts of bacon, *Geselchetes* (smoked pork), roast pork, sausages and cheese served on a wooden platter.

Bruckfleisch: off-cuts of various types of meat, mostly offal.

Buchteln (*Wuchteln*): oven-baked dumplings made from yeast dough and filled with jam, usually served with vanilla custard (*Dukatenbuchteln, recipe page 100*).

Burenwurst (*Burenhäutl*): a type of coarse boiling sausage, sold at little street sausage stalls.

Buschenschank (*Straußwirtschaft*): *Heuriger* selling home-produced wine, recognizable by the bunch of pine, fir or spruce twigs (*Buschen*) hanging outside.

Busserl: a very small, sweet biscuit (*Kokosbusserl*).

Butterschnitzel: veal rissole fried in butter.

Capers: buds of the caper bush. Preserved in vinegar, oil or saline solution, they will keep indefinitely.

Caraway seeds: a very popular flavouring in Austria, used in bread and biscuits and for seasoning meat and potato dishes.

Celeriac: mainly used in Austria for sauces and soups (*Suppengrün*), and as a vegetable or salad (*Selleriesalat*).

Ceps: rich-flavoured mushrooms. *See Box, page 34.*

Chervil: a herb with a sweet, aromatic flavour. The young leaves are used for sauces, soups, herb butter and salads. Found growing in almost every garden in Carinthia.

Chives: a member of the leek family, with long, thin, tubular leaves and an onion-like flavour. They are used raw in soups, sauces, salads, and fish and egg dishes. Essential ingredient in Austrian cuisine.

Clarified butter: butter clarified so that it can be used for frying at higher temperatures. To clarify butter, heat until melted and all bubbling stops. Remove from the heat and stand until the sediment has sunk to the bottom, then gently pour off the fat, straining it through muslin. Chill; use as required.

Cloves: spice used in both sweet and savoury dishes. *See Note, page 128.*

Coconut oil/butter: produced from the oil of the seeds of the coconut palm, this snow-white fat has a pleasant, nutty taste and is good for deep-frying as it can tolerate high cooking temperatures. *See also Note, page 42.*

Dalken (*Liwanzen*): small, thick pancakes made from yeast dough.

Debreziner: type of sausage similar to a frankfurter or Vienna sausage.

Einspänner: black coffee served with cream and icing sugar.

Eintropfsuppe: beef broth into which small pieces of dough made from flour, egg white and salt are dropped.

Faschiertes: minced meat.

Fiaker: black coffee served with a dash of kirsch or rum, decorated with a cherry.

Fleckerln: small squares of pasta shapes, used as a garnish for beef broth (*Schinkenfleckerln, recipe page 76*).

Frittaten: thin, unsweetened pancake, cut into strips and served in soup.

Geselchtes: smoked pork.

Gespritzter (*Gspritzter*): white wine diluted with mineral water or soda.

Gugelhupf: also known as *Kugelhopf*. Ring-shaped cake made with or without yeast, baked in a special fluted mould (*Kaisergugelhupf, recipe page 120*).

Hamburg parsley root: a popular root vegetable used in soups and meat dishes in Austrian cuisine. It looks like a small parsnip and tastes like a combination of parsnip, parsley and celery. *See also Note, page 53.*

Heuriger: young, recently harvested wine. The same name is given to inns serving the new wine.

Hollerstrauben: elderberry flowers deep-fried in batter.

Horseradish (*Kren*): the root of a cruciferous plant, used cooked in hot and cold sauces, usually to accompany beef, or grated raw to go with meat, fish and sausages. It is also available as a sauce in tubes or jars.

Jause: the name for a between-meals snack served at any time of day, sometimes with coffee.

Juniper berries: the blue-black berries of the juniper bush, usually sold dry. They are used to flavour sauces, fish and game dishes, and sauerkraut, and are also used for making schnapps.

Kaffee verkehrt: small mocha coffee topped with frothy hot milk.

Kaisermelange: large mocha without milk, mixed with egg yolk, honey and cognac or brandy.

Kaisersemmel: a round bread roll, with a characteristic pattern of five crescent shapes on top.

Kapuziner: small mocha with a few drops of cream.

Kaminwurz: piquant, smoked, hard sausage (the name means "smoked in the fireplace"), a speciality of the Tyrol.

Kärtner würstel: small, air-dried and cured sausage containing pork, garlic, saltpetre and coarsely ground pepper.

Katzenschroa: shreds of different kinds of meat and offal.

Kipfler: variety of waxy potato, long and curved in shape, good for use in salads.

Kletzenbrot: fruit loaf made from dried fruit and nuts (*recipe, page 124*).

Knödel: dumplings.

Koch: a sweet pudding, such as *Kipfelkoch* or *Salzburger Koch* (*recipe, page 116*).

Konsul: mocha with dash of cream.

Krainer würstel: small sausage in which the pork is partly minced, partly diced, seasoned with garlic and cold smoked.

Krapfen: round, slightly-flattened doughnuts made from yeast dough and deep-fried (*Faschingskrapfen, recipe page 132*).

Kuchen: cake.

Landjäger: hard, flat, highly-seasoned dry sausage.

Lovage: southern European herb. The fresh leaves are used sparingly in soups, sauces and ragouts. Lovage is especially popular in Carinthia.

Marend(e): an afternoon snack, mainly in the Tyrol and Vorarlberg.

Marjoram: herb widely used in Austrian cuisine. Dried marjoram is added to meat dishes, vegetables, ragouts, sausages, sauces, soups and potato dishes.

Melange: coffee with hot milk.

Nockerln: small pieces of dough shaped into dumplings which are added to soup or served as an accompaniment.

Nudeln: noodles.

Nutmeg: the fruit of the tropical nutmeg tree is an important spice in Austrian cookery. Freshly grated nutmeg is added to fish, meat and vegetable dishes.

Obers: whipping cream. *Kafeeobers* and *Teeobers* are low-fat versions.

Pafesen: also called *Pavesen* or *Pofesen*. Two slices of white bread sandwiched together with a sweet or savoury filling and deep-fried.

Palatschinken: paper-thin rolled pancakes (*Pfannkuchen*) with a sweet or savoury filling (*recipe, page 112*).

Panadelsuppe: beef soup garnished with pieces of white bread.

Paradeiser: tomatoes.

Parsley: Austrian cookery's most popular and widely-used culinary herb, The smooth leaves of flat-leaf parsley have a stronger flavour, while the crinkly type is milder but more decorative.

Patzerlgugelhupf: a ring-shaped cake, containing poppy seeds, nuts and quark (*recipe, page 121*).

Pogatscherln: savoury pastry made from potato or yeast dough, found mainly in Lower Austria.

Potize: strudel pastry made with yeast, filled with nuts or poppy seeds.

Poularden: fattened chickens with white juicy flesh. The tender *Poularden* of southern Styria are especially famous.

Powidl: plum purée. *See Note, page 98.*

Preßwurst: pig's head, feet and rind, mixed with leek, carrot, celeriac and parsley and made into brawn.

Punschkrapferl: small, cube-shaped sponge cakes covered with icing.

Quargel: small, round strong cheese.

Quark (*Topfen*)**:** a soft, acid-curd cheese with a mild, slightly sour flavour, which is used extensively in Austrian cooking. *See also Box, page 113.*

Rahm: cream or soured cream. In Viennese recipes *Rahm* always means soured cream.

Riebel (*Stopfer*)**:** crumbled, sautéed semolina, a speciality of Vorarlberg (*recipe, page 110*).

Riesling: dry white wine.

Ritscher(t): stew containing hulled barley, smoked meat and pulses, popular in Carinthia and Styria.

Rostbraten: top rib or leg of beef: strongly flavoured, fibrous beef marbled with fat.

Saffron: the dark orange and red dried stigmas of the saffron crocus and the world's most expensive spice. A very popular ingredient in Austrian cookery, it imparts a brilliant yellow colouring and is used to flavour meat soups (*Gailtaler Kirchtagssuppe, recipe page 28*) and fish dishes, and is also added to rice, sauces and pastry. It can also be bought in powdered form.

Sauerkraut: fermented shredded cabbage.

Saumeisen: a rural speciality from the Waldviertel area of Lower Austria. Minced lean pork, diced onion, garlic, salt, pepper and herbs are shaped into pieces about the size of a fist, stuffed into a pig's stomach, then slowly dried and smoked.

Schilcher: fresh, dry, mildly acidic, light rosé wine, a speciality of Styria.

Schill: a freshwater fish of the pike-perch family, also known as *Donauschill, Zander* or *Fogosch*. In Austria, they are usually fished from the Danube. Tender, succulent and pleasant tasting.

Schinken: ham.

Schmankerl: term for any kind of titbit, also a pudding made from flour, sugar, milk and cream.

Schöberl: pieces of savoury sponge used as a garnish for soups.

Schübling (*Schiebling*): sausage from Vorarlberg, similar to the small *Knackwurst* sausages popular in eastern Austria.

Schwarzer (small or large): black coffee.

Schwedenbombe: also known as *Mohrenkopf* or *Negerkuß*, a marshmallow on a wafer base, covered with chocolate.

Schnitzel: a very thin cut of meat, traditionally veal.

Schwein: pork.

Speck: bacon, boiled and smoked.

Sterz: purée made from flour, semolina or maize meal, fried in fat or cooked in water. *Türkensterz* is made from maize, and *Hadensterz* (sometimes called *Heidensterz*), from buckwheat flour.

Strauben: biscuits with a ridged surface made from yeast or choux pastry.

Strudel: pudding made from yeast, short or strudel pastry, filled with sliced apple, poppy seeds, nuts or quark, and rolled up. Also served as a savoury dish with a vegetable or meat filling. Strudel can be boiled or baked. S*ee Apple Strudel, recipe page 94; Quark Strudel, recipe page 96*).

Sturm: fermented grape juice.

Tarhonya: pasta originating from Hungary, mainly served as a side dish in the Burgenland region of Austria.

Tascherl (*Tascherl*): turnovers made from round pieces of pastry, filled and then folded in half (*Powidltascherln, recipe page 102*).

Thyme: herb originating in southern Europe, used dried for seasoning roast beef and game, fish, sauces and soups.

Tommerl (*Nigel, Nigl*): soufflé-like pudding found especially in Styria (*Apfeltommerl, Bluttommerl*).

Torte: round Viennese cake.

Verhackerte: finely chopped bacon spread, popular in Carinthia and Styria.

Verlängerter: small mocha, topped up with hot water to the volume of a large mocha.

Vintschgerl: rye biscuit made from two rounds of thin pastry joined together, a speciality of the Tyrol.

Windbäckerei: fluffy meringue made from egg white beaten with a little sugar until stiff.

Wurst: sausage.

Zwetschkenröster: plum compote boiled until all the juice has evaporated (*recipe, page 106*).

CONVERSION CHART

These figures are not exact equivalents, but have been rounded up or down slightly to make measuring easier.

Weight Equivalents		Volume Equivalents	
Metric	Imperial	Metric	Imperial
15 g	½ oz	8 cl	3 fl oz
30 g	1 oz	12.5 cl	4 fl oz
60 g	2 oz	15 cl	¼ pint
90 g	3 oz	17.5 cl	6 fl oz
125 g	¼ lb	25 cl	8 fl oz
150 g	5 oz	30 cl	½ pint
200 g	7 oz	35 cl	12 fl oz
250 g	½ lb	45 cl	¾ pint
350 g	¾ lb	50 cl	16 fl oz
500 g	1 lb	60 cl	1 pint
1 kg	2 to 2¼ lb	1 litre	35 fl oz

Cover: Pork fillet is roasted in the oven, then covered with a mixture of chopped mushrooms, onions, parsley and rosemary and encased in slices of ham and a golden puff-pastry crust (*recipe, page 66*). Served with baby carrots, chanterelle mushrooms in cream sauce (*recipe, page 84*), and new potatoes, it makes an elegant dish to serve for a dinner party or special occasion.

TIME-LIFE BOOKS

COOKERY AROUND THE WORLD
English edition staff for *Austria*
Editorial: Luci Collings, Felicity Jackson
Kate Cann, Charlotte Powell
Designer: Dawn McGinn
Production: Emma Wishart, Justina Cox
Technical Consultant: Michael A. Barnes

English translation by Isabel Varea for
Ros Schwartz Translations, London

Published originally under the title
Küchen der Welt: Österreich by Gräfe und
Unzer Verlag GmbH, Munich
© 1994 Gräfe und Unzer Verlag
GmbH, Munich

This edition published by Time-Life Books
B.V. Amsterdam
Authorized English language edition
© 1994 Time-Life Books B.V.
First English language printing 1994

TIME-LIFE is a trademark of Time Warner
Inc. U.S.A.

ISBN 0 7054 1203 2

GRÄFE UND UNZER

EDITORS: Dr. Stephanie von Werz-Kovacs
and Birgit Rademacker
Sub-Editor: Katharina Lisson
Designer: Konstantin Kern
Recipes tested by: Renate Neis
Production: Esta Denroche
Cartography: Huber, Munich

Adelheid Beyreder was born in Styria but has for many years lived in Vienna, where she manages a bookshop and indulges in her twin hobbies of travel and cookery—interests that date back to her childhood. In addition to amassing a large collection of cookery books, she collects, invents and tests recipes. For this book she has put together a selection of both familiar and less well-known authentic Austrian recipes.

Michael Brauner, who photographed the food for this volume, is a graduate of the Berlin Fotoschule. He worked as an assistant to several French and German photographers before setting up on his own in 1984. He now divides his time between his studios in Munich, Karlsruhe and Gordes in Provence.

Dietrich Ebert studied graphic design at the Academy of Fine Arts in Stuttgart. In 1982, after a period spent teaching at the University of Braunschwieg, he became a freelance illustrator and graphic designer. For this book he has devised an atmospheric series of illustrations that resemble tiny copperplate engravings.

Picture Credits

Colour illustrations: Dietrich Ebert

All photographs by Michael Brauner unless indicated below:

Cover: Graham Kirk, London. 4, top (Vienna's Naschmarkt): real bild, Klaus-D Neumann, Munich; centre (woodstacks outside a farmhouse): ai aigner impuls, Gottfried Aigner, Munich; bottom (flock of geese): Bildagentur J Dziemballa, Barbo, Munich. 4-5, top (hut in Zillertal), bottom (white house with apple trees): real bild, Klaus-D Neumann, Munich. 8-9 (Lienz Dolomites): real bild, Klaus-D Neumann, Munich. 10: ai aigner impuls, Gottfried Aigner, Munich. 11: Herbert Hartmann, Munich. 12, top: Bildagentur J Dziemballa, Munich; bottom: Werner Neumeister, Munich. 13: Bildagentur J Dziemballa, Barbo, Munich. 14: Pressebüro Franz Roth, Nuremberg. 15: ai aigner impuls, Gottfried Aigner, Munich. 16: Thomas Widmann, Regensburg. 17: Bildagentur J Dziemballa, Janicke, Munich. 18, bottom: Herbert Hartmann, Munich. 18, top, 19, 20: real bild, Klaus-D Neumann, Munich. 21 (2): Herbert Hartmann, Munich. 30: Bildagentur J Dziemballa, Barbo, Munich. 34: Hermann Rademacker, Munich. 41: Uli Franz, Cologne. 54, 90: Fotostudio Teubner, Füssen. 104: Friedrich Strauß, Au in de Hellertau. 108: real bild, Klaus-D Neumann, Munich. 131: Armin Faber, Mülheim.

Colour reproduction by Fotolito Longo, Bolzano, Italy
Typeset by A. J. Latham Limited, Dunstable, Bedfordshire, England
Printed and bound by Mondadori, Verona, Italy